THE IRISH HOME

THE IRISH HOME

ECLECTIC AND UNIQUE INTERIORS

photographs and text

IANTHE RUTHVEN

WITHDRAWN

RIZZOLI
NEW YORK

FOR SKIMPER
whose dogged encouragement and generous contributions
to the text brought the project to fruition.
Thank you.

First published in the United States of America in 1998 by
Rizzoli International Publications, Inc.
300 Park Avenue South
New York, NY 10010

First published in Great Britain in 1998 by
Collins & Brown Limited

ISBN 0-8478-2119-6
LC 98-65889

Editor: Alison Wormleighton
Designer: David Fordham

Typeset by MATS, Southend-on-Sea, Essex
Reproduction by Hong Kong Graphic & Printing
Printed and bound in Singapore by C. S. Graphics

HALF TITLE: *The upper landing at Ballinterry.*
FRONTISPIECE: *View of the main bedroom at*
Ballaghmore Castle, County Laois, a 1480s tower house
built by the Gaelic chieftain MacGiollaphadraig.
TITLE PAGE: *The summer drawing room at Capard.*

Acknowledgments

I would like to thank all those who welcomed me into their homes – often at very short notice – and patiently allowed me to turn them upside down in order to achieve photographs which I hope they will recognize. Everyone, as so often in Ireland, provided help and hospitality way beyond the call of common courtesy. Unfortunately, for reasons of space, not all the houses I visited and photographed could be included in this book: I am no less grateful to them for their help.

In addition, I would like to thank the following for their generous and informative contributions to the text: John Aboud, Phillipa Bayliss, Countess Anne and the late Count Gunnar Bernsdorff, Alfred Cochrane, Tom Dobson, Amanda Douglas, Olivia Durdin-Robertson, John Farrington, Anne Gatti, Cdr Bill King, Tarka King, Sir John Leslie, Bt, Samantha Leslie, Ian Lumley, Ruadhan McEoin, John McSweeney, Julian and Carola Peck, Sally Phipps, Sean Rafferty, Nick and Lima Groves Raines, Egerton Shelswell-White, Peter and Gillian Somerville-Large, Dorothy Walker and Gordon Watson.

A special thanks to Nicola Gordon Bowe, Patrick Bowe, the Hon Desmond and Penny Guinness, Marina Guinness, Claudia Kinmonth, John McBratney, Nabil Saidi and Jeremy Williams, who put me in touch with some of the people whose houses appear in this book. Many others who contributed energy, time, information and hospitality include: Dr Toby Barnard, Pauline Bewick, Paul Caffrey, Joanna Cramsey, Anthony Farrell, David FitzHerbert, Peter and Phyllis Fleming, Prof Roy Foster, the Hon Kieran and Vivienne Guinness, Ros Harvey and Tim Stampton, Simon Kenna, Vere Lenox-Conyngham, Michael Lynch, Peter Marson, Nicholas and Susan Mosse, Senator David Norris, Sir Michael and Lady Nugent, Noelle Campbell Sharp, Desirée Short, Pip Simmons, and Chris Wilson. Jackie Byrne at Primary Colour in Dublin provided an invaluable service.

Thanks to Cindy Richards and David Fordham at Collins & Brown for their patience and forbearance during the design and production process; and to Alison Wormleighton for helpful suggestions with the text.

And, most of all, my heartfelt thanks to Paul Keegan and Lizzie van Amerongen, whose continued support, encouragement and succour in Dublin and Kilkenny made everything possible.

Excerpt from "Settings" from *Seeing Things* by Seamus Heaney. Copyright © 1991 by Seamus Heaney. Reprinted by permission of Farrar, Straus & Giroux, Inc., New York, and Faber & Faber, London.

CONTENTS

RIGHT: *A stringless harp in the drawing room of 50 North Great Georges Street, Dublin.*

OVERLEAF: *The hall at Ballinterry with the music room in the background.*

INTRODUCTION

OPPOSITE: *Flamboyantly painted ottages in County Cork, where bright colours and a certain artistic exuberance are a common feature. Most are on the Beara Peninsula, where whole villages are painted amazing colours.*
RIGHT: *A traditional two-tone Irish dresser, with bars to support plates.*

THE ELUSIVE QUALITIES OF THE IRISH home have been celebrated more lastingly in literature than in photography. For a people who so often have been driven into exile by political or economic necessity, the ancestral home, be it castle or cottage, exerts a powerful appeal. The home in the mind can be so much more durable than bricks or stones, furniture or draperies. For most of us the value we find in material objects has less to do with aesthetics than with associations.

The houses in this book have been chosen because each in its different way has managed to preserve or communicate something about these absent presences. Although the popular idea of traditional Irishness may still reside in the postcard clichés of thatched cottages or Norman banqueting halls, a sense of Irishness that corresponds to lived experience is a good deal harder to pin down. It is not so much the result of the evolution or consistent application of a particular vernacular style Instead, it derives from the way that styles borrowed from others have been domesticated and translated into rich and variegated modes of self-expression.

History and culture have everything to do with this process. Prior to the Norman invasion in 1066, England already had been subjected to a millennium of road-building and urbanization. But before the Norman invasion of Ireland, more than a century later, the country knew little of domestic architecture. The first towns – Limerick, Waterford, Dublin and Cork – began as Viking forts; the Normans built magnificent castles, and gradually the fortified stronghold, or tower house, such as Oranmore (*qv*) in Galway, established itself (especially in the turbulent West) as the base from which the Norman–Gaelic chieftains exercised dominion and patronage.

By the end of the Middle Ages the Irish had won back most of their land, but over the next few centuries the English confiscated Irish property and gave it to "planted" Protestants from England and Scotland. In the late seventeenth century the Irish revolted, supporting the Catholic James II against the Protestant William of Orange, who had supplanted James on the throne. The Williamite wars culminated in an Irish defeat in 1690 at the Battle of the Boyne, completing the pattern of conquest and settlement that had begun with the Norman invasion. The native aristocracy, comprising the Gaelic clans and some of the Anglo–Normans who had become partially assimilated, paid a crushing historical price for backing James II. Many fled abroad, to offer their military skills to England's enemies: over the next half-century, 150,000 Irishmen died in the service of France. Few countries can ever have had to bear such a loss of native aristocracy.

As the reformed religion became associated with the new political order, the lines of division were drawn not so much between Irish and English as between Catholic and Protestant. "In the new aristocracy of self-made men," writes Peter Somerville-Large, "every rank and position was open so long as a man was Protestant. Anyone with aspirations to prosperity was tempted to turn and modest Papist landowners could retain their possessions if they changed their religion." The echo of conquest survives in names like Castletown, Castlecoole and Castle Leslie, none of them fortified strongholds but country mansions built as expressions of power.

The contrast with England is striking. As the Irish novelist Molly Keane has pointed out, English country houses, both great and small, "have an air of blessed permanence. They sit low in their wooded valleys, comfortable as cups in saucers." Their Irish counterparts, however, "are ethereal in their uselessness, and

INTRODUCTION

LEFT: *This three-tiered wooden plate rack was in Ballinterry when Hurd Hatfield bought the house, and is now used to store plates in the dining room.*

RIGHT: *The kitchen at the Glebe House in County Donegal, formerly the home of the painter Derek Hill and now a museum and gallery. It has changed little over the years, except for the occasional coat of paint on the dresser.*

ABOVE: *The huge eighteenth-century dresser in the old kitchen at Newbridge House, with an array of items essential to the smooth running of a large country house.*

LEFT: *An old Irish dresser in a* cottage orné *at Kilfane, County Kilkenny.*

extravagant in the spaces their designers yielded to one object only – beauty", a beauty, one might add, intended as much to intimidate and impress as to allure.

The first chapter, Militant Grandeur, explores this theme. Castletown, the largest and still the grandest of the great Irish houses, was the brainchild of William Conolly. One of the most successful of those self-made Irishmen of the Protestant Ascendancy, Conolly took full advantage of being on the winning side, and constructed from the profits of forfeited Catholic estates a mansion he considered suitable for his new station in life as Speaker of the all-Protestant Irish Parliament. As the historian Roy Foster has noted, the very extravagance of such projects betrayed an underlying feeling of insecurity. "The Ascendancy built in order to convince themselves not only that they had arrived, but that they would remain." The folly of such enterprises – from a strictly practical viewpoint – is exemplified by Castlecoole, a neoclassical gem whose construction out of the finest imported materials all but bankrupted its owner, the first Earl of Belmore. At Newbridge, seat of an archbishop, the wealth of the Church of Ireland – the moral authority underpinning Ascendancy power – is displayed in richly decorated doorcases and ornate rococo ceilings.

Romantic Elegance, the second chapter, aims to capture the distinctive style of opulence and exuberance that characterized the Anglo–Irish vision in the high summer of the Ascendancy when earlier insecurities had been temporarily allayed, if not forgotten. Anglo–Irish grandees, desirous of keeping up appearances before their wealthier cousins across the water, indulged their fantasies to the full. There is, perhaps, in such extravagance an echo of the old Gaelic spirit, combined with the underlying though unacknowledged sense that nemesis might soon be at hand. And indeed, for many, nemesis arrived in the shape of the Great Famine of the mid-nineteenth century, when many of their tenants either died of starvation or emigrated, and later the Wyndham Acts, which broke up the large estates. A different kind of elegance, more considered and less flamboyant, is exhibited in the eighteenth

century Gothicized interior of Leixlip Castle. Here, the finest Irish furniture is offset against strong but subtle colours, creating a rare example of a castle continuously cherished and inhabited since Norman times.

Chapter Three, Sweet Disorder, is a celebration of what the early eighteenth-century Irish judge and politician Sir Jonah Barrington in his memoirs called the "cult of dilapidation" – though these pictures will hopefully testify to what talent and ingenuity can achieve regardless of financial constraints. The owner of Ballinterry, Hurd Hatfield, is an American without obvious Irish connections, but, like other compatriots, he has found in an old Irish house the perfect theatre in which to play host to "absent presences" from the past. In their County Mayo bungalow Anthony and Michael Coyle, the "Birdmen of Mullet", have created a masterpiece of folk art that deserves to be celebrated. The seventeenth-century Huntington Castle – which was chosen by the director Stanley Kubrick as the setting for his film *Barry Lyndon* – is in a class of its own. The basement of this house filled with fading tapestries and elegant plasterwork ceilings is devoted to religious practices not seen in Ireland since St Patrick banished the snakes and demons.

Versions of the Pastoral, the fourth chapter, seeks out some of the more remote country retreats where traditional vernacular dwellings have been restored or repaired. At Bothar Bui, in a wild and beautiful part of west Cork, the late Robin Walker and his wife, Dorothy, restored two cabins, possibly dating from the seventeenth century, which now form part of a hillside hamlet overlooking an ancient oak wood, with dramatic views of the mountains known as MacGillycuddy's Reeks. Robin's discreetly functional modern structures blend well with the rugged whitewashed walls of the old stone cabins. At Ballynabrocky in County Wicklow the artist Patrick Scott has restored a traditional "two-up, two-down" farmhouse, and filled it with simple cottage furniture, some of it so unappreciated that he acquired it for free. A cottage on the island of Gola, off the Donegal coast, is a tribute to the persistence and ingenuity of Nick and Limma Groves Raines, who over

the years have braved storms and gales to restore and preserve for posterity one of several cottages deserted by the islanders more than thirty years ago. The Mellon Cottage in the Ulster Folk Museum recalls the hearth that once lay at the centre of Irish life, before it was replaced by the ubiquitous modern bungalow with picture windows and central heating. The improvements in comfort have not been achieved without cost. The poet Seamus Heaney once observed that those who remember the closing of open hearths in country kitchens and their replacement, first by bandy-legged iron stoves and then by radiators indiscriminately placed around the walls, "have already inscribed in the memory-bank of their bodies a record of the almost physical consequences which one's being suffered in the process of modernization. . . . Any hearth was all the hearths there had ever been. Every morning . . . the primal flame was gratefully rekindled. Fast-forward . . . to the central heating system, and abruptly you have the cancellation of wonder."

The skill of the modern restorer is to preserve the sense of the past, conveyed in spaces and settings, while being faithful to the present with the demands it makes on comfortable living. The increase in wealth and the improvements in the quality of life engendered by

Ireland's participation in the European Union have created many opportunities for reviving old buildings. Chapter Five, Restoration and Revival, shows some of the best examples of imagination and creativity working with the grain of old buildings without slavishly recreating the past. Tom Dobson has brought back to life Capard, a fine early nineteenth-century Ascendancy house in County Laois. At Prehen, Julian and Carola Peck have lovingly restored the ancestral home of the Knoxes, using strong colours to enhance its architectural qualities. At Corke Lodge, Alfred Cochrane has created a series of playful post-modern variations around the classical-versus-Gothic theme created by the Irish Regency architect James Shiel.

Anyone glancing through this book might reasonably ask what its unifying theme could be. Ireland is a country where individualism thrives at the expense of slavery to fashion. This sense of freedom is extended, like Irish hospitality, to anyone who comes to the island. Many talents nurtured abroad find in Ireland the opportunity to express themselves without the constraints that might have limited them elsewhere. However different the houses, in size and function, they seem to share one common feature: their owners have had the courage to follow their instincts.

GRANDEUR

CASTLETOWN

OPPOSITE: *The staircase hall leading through to the entrance hall, designed by Sir Edward Lovett Pearce. The cantilevered staircase and stucco decoration by the Swiss–Italian Francini brothers, like most of the interior, were commissioned by Lady Louisa Conolly. Three of the banisters are signed and dated by their maker, "A King, Dublin 1760".*

LEFT: *The entrance façade from the west colonnade. The central block of three storeys over a basement resembles a Renaissance town palazzo. The wings were designed in the Palladian style by Sir Edward Lovett Pearce, who supervised the work in its later stages. In the manner of some Italian Palladian villas, they incorporate the stables and servants' quarters.*

BUILT IN 1719–32 FOR WILLIAM CONOLLY, Castletown, in County Kildare, was Ireland's first and largest Palladian mansion. "I am glad for the honour of my country," wrote Sir John Perceval to his friend, the Church of Ireland bishop and philosopher George Berkeley, "that Mr. Conolly has undertaken so magnificent a pile of building, and your advice has been taken upon it . . . for since this house will be the finest Ireland ever saw, and by your description fit for a Prince, I would have it as it were the epitome of the Kingdom, and all the natural rarities she afford should have a place there."

Though the design has been credited to the Florentine architect Alessandro Galilei, with the wings by Sir Edward Lovett Pearce, it might just as well have been lifted from the *Vitruvius Britannicus* (a three-volume book of architectural designs published in 1715, 1717 and 1725, and highly influential in launching the Palladian revival), in which several English houses of similar design are illustrated. Its larger proportions, however, may reflect an underlying sense of insecurity and a need to impress. William Conolly, who was Speaker of the Irish House of Commons from 1715 until his death in 1729, had risen from humble origins in Donegal. He had become one of the most powerful magnates in the land, mainly by dealing in estates forfeited by Catholics during the Williamite wars. His house – an outsize Italian palazzo, deposited on the banks of the Liffey west of Dublin, with wings to accommodate stables and servants – sends out a message of grandeur tinged with menace. It is a political manifesto in stone.

RIGHT: *In the eighteenth century the long gallery was used as a living room, with "fine glasses, books, musical instruments and a billiard table", according to Lady Caroline Dawson, who visited in 1778. The central niche contains a seventeenth-century statue of the goddess Diana. The glass chandelier is one of three, all specially made in Venice for Castletown.*

ABOVE: *The long gallery was redecorated with frescoes in the Pompeian manner in the 1770s by Lady Louisa Conolly.*

18

MILITANT
GRANDEUR

CASTLETOWN

RIGHT: *The green drawing room, redecorated in the 1760s, was the principal reception room. The chairs flanking the lacquer cabinet are Irish and come from Headford House, County Meath.*
BELOW: *The print room, created by Lady Louisa, is the only one in Ireland that survives from the eighteenth century.*

William Conolly never lived to see his project completed and, following his widow's death in 1752, Castletown passed to his great-nephew, Tom Conolly. It was Tom's wife, Lady Louisa Conolly, daughter of the Duke of Richmond, who set her stamp on the interior. The print room she created was probably the first in Ireland. Lady Louisa's improvements were doubtless influenced by sibling rivalry. Her sister Emily, Duchess of Leinster, presided over Carton a short distance away and produced twenty-three children before committing the social disgrace of marrying her children's tutor only a year after her husband's death. Louisa was childless – Castletown was her child. In her dying moments she had a tent erected on the lawn so she could take one last, lingering look.

The house remained in the hands of William Conolly's descendants until 1967. It was rescued from almost certain demolition by Desmond Guinness, founder of the Irish Georgian Society, who opened it to the public.

ABOVE: *The red damask French wall coverings in the drawing room date from the 1820s. The writing cabinet was made for Lady Louisa in the 1760s. To the left hangs a portrait of Thomas, Earl of Louth, and on the right a late eighteenth-century portrait of an unknown lady.*

MILITANT
GRANDEUR

CASTLECOOLE

ABOVE: *Set in beautiful parkland, Castlecoole is a masterpiece of neoclassical design. The four giant Ionic columns supporting the central portico are echoed b colonnades of fluted Doric columns ending in Doric pavilions.*
OPPOSITE: *The drawing room viewed from the oval saloon shows the high quality of the joinery and stucco. The gilt torchères flanking the doors are part of the Regency suite made especially for this room.*

THE MOST PALATIAL LATE EIGHTEENTH-CENTURY house in Ireland, Castlecoole in County Fermanagh aptly expresses the aspirations of its creator, Armar Lowry Corry, first Earl of Belmore. "It was to be the home of a great Irish political family," says the historian Dr Anthony Malcomson, "not merely a place to live in but a showpiece to proclaim Belmore's position in Irish society and influence in the Irish House of Commons." Unfortunately for Belmore his timing for this grandiose project could not have been worse. Within just a few years of the house's completion in 1797 the Irish Parliament had been abolished and its powers transferred to London. Belmore, as an opponent of the Union, lost most of his political influence. Afflicted with rheumatism and gout, he retired to Bath, leaving his son, Somerset, Viscount Corry, to face the consequences of the family's political marginalization.

PREVIOUS PAGES: *A hall ought to "express the dignity of its possessor", according to Thomas Sheraton. Here, James Wyatt created a hall of great depth using the same stone as for the exterior, adorned only with a plain Doric frieze and columns of porphyry scagliola.*

RIGHT: *Carved and gilded sofas and chairs, rosewood tables and pier glasses in the drawing room are splendid examples of Regency furniture. The portraits on the end wall show (left) the first Earl of Belmore and (right) his wife, Lady Margaret Butler. In the centre is Elizabeth Corry (1715–91), the first Earl's aunt.*

OPPOSITE: *The oval saloon with its scagliola pilasters seen from the drawing room. Due to the cost of construction the interior decoration had to wait twenty years and was undertaken by the second Earl at a staggering cost of fifty thousand pounds. The Regency furnishings were mostly supplied by John Preston, a leading Dublin upholsterer.*

Like Conolly's Castletown (*qv*), Castlecoole's impressive size reflects its builder's meteoric social rise – in this case from plain Mr Lowry Corry, scion of a family of Belfast linen merchants, through Baron and Viscount Belmore, to Earl of Belmore in 1797. It is, however, noticeably smaller than Castletown (with only two storeys and nine bays in the central block to Castletown's three storeys and thirteen bays). Perhaps this reflects the greater assurance the Protestant Ascendancy had acquired.

Belmore insisted on building his house out of materials imported from England. Not content with the original Palladian designs by Richard Johnston, an Irishman, he employed the fashionable English architect James Wyatt who, much influenced by Stuart and Revett's *Antiquities of Athens* (published in 1762), gave the house its massive and restrained Grecian feel. No expense was spared. The beautifully cut masonry in Portland stone was shipped to Ballyshannon in Donegal, taken overland to Lough Erne, shipped again to Enniskillen and transported the last part of the journey by bullock cart. English plasterers were brought over under the supervision of Joseph Rose.

When Lord Belmore died in 1802 he left debts amounting to seventy thousand pounds; his great house had cost nearly twice the original estimate of thirty thousand pounds. No one has ever quite worked out whether the exceptionally restrained interior design is a perfect expression of neoclassical elegance or the result of a shortage of funds. In 1951 Castlecoole was acquired by the National Trust, which has spent more than three million pounds on restoring the masonry and interior.

MILITANT GRANDEUR

NEWBRIDGE HOUSE

OPPOSITE: *A stone-flagged vestibule provides an open space adjoining the inner hall of Newbridge House. The richly pedimented gilded doorcase framed by fluted columns and Corinthian capitals makes for a highly theatrical entrance to the red drawing room. Some of the urns and statues came from Heywood House in County Laois.*

LEFT: *Newbridge House in its parkland demesne, one of the finest examples of eighteenth-century landscape design in Ireland. The identity of the landscape gardener who laid out the grounds is uncertain, but records dating from 1776 suggest it may have been Charles Frizell, from a well-known firm of Wexford land-surveyors.*

"A TRUE BISHOP," WROTE THEOPHILUS BOLTON, an Anglican cleric who became Archbishop of Cashel, "has nothing more to do than eat, drink, grow fat [and] rich, and die." With comparatively few parishioners to look after – only twenty-five per cent of the overall population was Protestant, and many of these were dissenters – the Anglican clergy were an essential part of the eighteenth-century Ascendancy. Senior members were able to benefit from the rich endowments enjoyed by the established church. One such was Charles Cobbe. Arriving from England in 1717 as chaplain to his cousin, the Lord Lieutenant, he eventually rose to become Archbishop of Dublin. In 1737 – already firmly ensconced on the ladder of ecclesiastical preferment as Bishop of Kildare – he commissioned his friend George Semple to design a handsome yet sober villa for him on his Newbridge demesne, at Donabate, north of Dublin.

On his death in 1765 the estate passed to his second son, Thomas, who married an heiress, Lady Elizabeth Beresford (known as Lady Betty), daughter of the Earl of Tyrone, and the most fashionable woman in Dublin. Addicted to entertaining on a lavish scale, the couple added a vast drawing room which was used as a picture gallery to house their collection of Old Masters. These had been purchased on their behalf by the Reverend Matthew Pilkington, vicar of Donabate church and author of the first English-language dictionary of painters. During the era of Lady Betty and "Old Tommie", as her husband

OPPOSITE: *Looking into the inner hall from the vestibule. On the back wall hangs a portrait of members of the Powerscourt family. Lord Powerscourt was godfather to one of "Old Tommie" and Lady Betty's children. A marble statue of wrestlers stands on an Irish Georgian breakfast table.*

RIGHT: *Shells, marine instruments and hundreds of other trophies are displayed in the Museum of Curiosities at Newbridge House. Family museums were not uncommon in the eighteenth century but this collection is one of very few to have survived.*

was known, carriageloads of relatives and their servants filled the house, and large quantities of liquor were consumed between bouts of fox-hunting and card-playing. A keen amateur physician, Lady Betty cured her guests' ailments with her own special recipe for tar-water: it started with six gallons of brandy.

In later generations the Cobbes would prove much less flamboyant and possibly more Christian than their ecclesiastical forebear and his son. In the 1830s Thomas's grandson, Charles, sold two landscapes by Hobbema and Poussin to pay for eighty cottages for tenants on his estate in the Dublin mountains. They became known as the Hobbema Cottages. In his diary, which survives along with a virtually complete collection of estate accounts and inventories covering two centuries, Charles Cobbe reasoned that the Hobbema hung in a dark corner, hardly noticed by those who saw it. A far better picture to delight Christian eyes would be warm, dry, stone cottages for his tenants.

RIGHT: *The red drawing room was added around 1760. The rococo ceiling presides over a coordinated scheme of carpet, wallpaper and curtains, a rare survival from the nineteenth century.*

ABOVE: *A Victorian head stands on a late-Georgian marble-topped eagle console table in the red drawing room. The table is one of a pair with matching pier glasses, made by Irish craftsmen.*

OPPOSITE: *The picture above the table is a studio copy of Bernardo Strozzi's painting* The Musicians, *the original version of which is in Hampton Court Palace, near London. Much of the furniture in the red drawing room was supplied by Dublin craft firms such as Mack, William & Gibton, who also made the curtains.*

In her memoirs recalling Anglo–Irish life before the Great Famine, Charles's wife, Frances Cobbe, described the stifling atmosphere of high-minded Christian paternalism prevailing at Newbridge during Charles's time. When tenants arrived they were given platefuls of meat and jugs of beer which had to be consumed out of doors. "When anyone was born or married, or ill or dead, or going to America, embassies were always sent to Newbridge seeking assistance." In cases of death, the bereaved were given pots of jam. To the last, Frances found that "the connection between dying and wanting raspberry jam remained a mystery". Indoors, "clocks and bells and gongs sounded regularly for prayers and meals". Charles resented such innovations as "the atrocious and disgraceful practice of afternoon tea".

Like other Anglo–Irish families, the economic power of the Cobbes declined drastically after the Great Famine. Frances recalled the day the potato blight arrived at Newbridge, in July 1845. "As we passed a remarkably fine field of potatoes in full blossom the scent came in through the open windows of the carriage and we remarked to each other how splendid was the crop. Three or four hours later, as we returned home in the dark, a dreadful smell came from the same field. Next morning there was a wail from one end of Ireland to the other."

In 1985, when the Cobbe family finally decided to sell Newbridge, it was bought by Dublin County Council under a unique arrangement that enables the family to use part of the house in exchange for leaving the furniture and furnishings on permanent loan.

THREE DUBLIN HOUSES

OPPOSITE: *No 7 Henrietta Street was built in 1733 by the architect Nathaniel Clements, who lived there until he died in 1777. The handsome classical stair hall includes the interior window from which his wife – "finer than the finest lady in England", according to the well-known observer Mrs Delany (an Englishwoman who lived in Ireland for over twenty years) – could inspect visitors without being seen.*

LEFT: *One of the neoclassical plaster figurines, with a maize-motif surround, in the dining parlour of No 50 North Great Georges Street. Taken from an eighteenth-century book of engravings called Classical Gems, there were originally eight such roundels, probably added c1790, some years after the main body of rococo plasterwork was completed.*

A N AMERICAN TOURIST WHO VISITED DUBLIN early in the nineteenth century found that it presented "the most extraordinary contrast of poverty and magnificence to be met with in Europe". The approach lay through suburbs of miserable hovels, where half-naked children clad in filthy rags huddled against muddy walls. But on reaching the centre he imagined himself to be "in one of the most elegant cities in Europe . . . There is no part of London which can compare with the centre of Dublin in beauty and magnificence."

Like the great country houses with their ostentatious Palladian façades, eighteenth-century Dublin, extending far beyond the limits of the old city founded by the Vikings in the tenth century, was designed to impress. The fine streets and squares of central Dublin, with their generous proportions, owe their existence to the Wide Streets Commission established in 1757, but large-scale speculation in north Dublin preceded that by several decades. Construction was often planned in a gap-toothed way: enough ground would be released for an individual to build two or three houses – one for himself and the others for letting. English visitors, especially Londoners, were amazed by the grandeur of what they had expected to be a provincial town. Most of the fabric of what was sometimes described as the "second city in Europe" survived, decaying but intact, until the 1960s, when parts of it were torn down by the developers, abetted by Irish governments that still saw in Dublin's handsome Georgian streets the symbols of colonial rule.

RIGHT: *The ante-room adjoining the drawing room at No 12 Henrietta Street, built in 1730 to the design of Sir Edward Lovett Pearce and now owned by Ian Lumley. A bust of William Pitt the Younger stands on a Regency console table.*

ABOVE: *The drawing room showing the horizontal sub-divisions carried out after 1887, when the building was turned into tenements.*

ABOVE: *Another view of
the ante-room at No 12
Henrietta Street showing
the slope where the early
nineteenth-century
staircase was.*

RIGHT: *Detail of the
dining parlour at No 50
North Great Georges
Street, showing a roundel
with garlands and bay-leaf
swags above a sideboard
with modern Turkish
Yildiz ware bowls.*

OPPOSITE: *An early
nineteenth-century
portrait of a French judge
hangs above a wooden
mantelpiece in the
drawing room of No 50
North Great Georges
Street. Nabil Saidi bought
the house in 1989 and is
undertaking a painstaking
restoration project.
During most of the
twentieth century the
house was tenemented.*

The grandest street in north Dublin was Henrietta Street, probably named after
Henrietta, Duchess of Grafton. Its builder, Luke Gardiner, was a highly successful
banker and speculator, and by the mid-nineteenth century his descendants owned a
sizeable chunk of north Dublin. Henrietta Street and nearby North Great Georges Street
held their own long after rival centres of social attraction had been created: a 1792
directory lists one archbishop, two bishops, four peers and four MPs among the residents
of Henrietta Street. However, after the Act of Union in 1801, abolishing the Irish
Parliament, the social status of Dublin's North Side began to decline. The city's Victorian
élite preferred to reside around the verdant precincts of Merrion Square and St Stephen's
Green, south of the River Liffey. The North Side reached its nadir in the mid-twentieth
century, by which time many of the finest houses had been reduced to slums. A few
enthusiasts are now restoring individual houses to their former glory.

ELEGANCE

LEIXLIP CASTLE

OPPOSITE: *Upstairs landing with a phaeton. The main staircase and landing were added around 1720 by filling in part of the courtyard. Rooms and passages were panelled, concealing the last vestiges of medieval roughness, and converting the castle into the comfortable, civilized home it remains today.*

LEFT: *Leixlip Castle was built as a square defensible block by Norman invaders in the 1170s. The alterations in the first half of the eighteenth century by the Conolly family of Castletown (qv) gave the castle a fashionably Gothic look by adding windows with pointed arches and glazing bars decorated with diamond patterning. More windows might have been added if the thickness of the walls had not made the task so difficult.*

IN A COUNTRY WHERE MOST ANCIENT CASTLES have been reduced to crumbling ruins, Leixlip in County Kildare is an outstanding exception. Desmond Guinness, a member of Ireland's illustrious brewing dynasty, acquired the castle with his wife, Mariga, in 1958. The village had a special significance: it was here that the family fortune was founded after Archbishop Price of Dublin, who died in 1762, bequeathed two hundred pounds to his servant, Richard Guinness, and Richard's son, Arthur. According to family tradition Archbishop Price also passed on the secret recipe for brewing a very dark beer, his favourite "porter". The recipe was to prove far more valuable than the money.

Although Desmond inherited a share in the business and an affection for the town, he lacked the worldly goods to fill such an imposing property as Leixlip. "As the second in a family of eleven," he says, "I had no furniture or pictures of my own." With Mariga he scoured the galleries and auction houses for Irish pictures and furniture. "What a moment it was to hunt the sale rooms!" he recalls. "Country houses were selling up left and right, and large pieces were going for a song." At one Dublin sale he paid twenty-five shillings for what he thought would make a nice kitchen table. A good scrubbing revealed a fine mahogany Irish table with grotesque masks and a black marble top – a rare Georgian find.

Co-founders of the revived Irish Georgian Society in 1958, Desmond and Mariga shamed the Irish government and public into doing something about the country's

OPPOSITE TOP: *A mirror by Booker of Dublin hangs above the dressing table in the blue bedroom.*
OPPOSITE BELOW: *The shell bedroom, where arch-shaped bedheads echo Leixlip's Gothic windows.*
BELOW: *A portrait by the eighteenth-century Irish painter Nathaniel Hone hangs over the fireplace in the blue bedroom.*

magnificent eighteenth-century heritage. Great mansions like Castletown (*qv*) and swathes of Georgian Dublin such as Mountjoy Square were in danger of being destroyed by the developers and their hatchet men. Some country houses were even pulled down just for the lead on their roofs. Unlike in England and Northern Ireland, where the National Trust existed to save the nation's architectural heritage, the Irish government had few resources for conservation. Given the legacy of bitterness and suspicion towards the former ruling class that lasted long after the South achieved political independence, politicians were inclined to devote such resources as were available to restoring round towers and ancient abbeys rather than Ascendancy demesnes.

With Leixlip as their showpiece, the Guinnesses initiated a new Irish country house style. The chintzes, pastel shades and fussy tassels of interiors on both sides of the Irish Sea during the 1950s were replaced by a new, specifically Irish look. Heavily carved eighteenth-century Irish furniture was set against strong but subtle colours. "This was a highly architectural style that respected the structure of interiors; windows were left uncurtained, layers of flaking paintwork left untouched and furniture left unrestored," writes art historian Paul Caffrey. "This new aesthetic of the informal, unrestored yet grand interior was well suited to Irish houses that had been neglected for generations."

OPPOSITE: *The dolls'
house in the drawing room
was originally made for
Newbridge House (qv).*
LEFT: *The gilded plaster
frieze in the library and the
engravings pasted on to the
walls are eighteenth-
century. The portrait is of
Desmond Guinness's
mother, Diana Mitford.*
BELOW: *The stair hall
dates from about 1720.*

RIGHT: *A Victorian copper bathtub sits in the window of King John's room, where the Norman king is said once to have slept. The four-poster came from Stowe House in England. The cover is embroidered with shamrocks and the slogan* Erin go bragh *("Ireland for ever!").*

OPPOSITE: *The front hall is paved with terracotta tiles and white flagstones. The fireplace, of black Kilkenny marble, came from Ardgillan Castle, County Dublin, and dates from around 1740. The quartered coat-of-arms is from a tomb of the Gorges family in County Meath.*

Mariga Guinness, who died in 1990, had an exceptional talent for colour schemes and used fabrics brilliantly. The designer David Mlinaric, a regular visitor to Leixlip during the 1960s, says, "She showed what could be done with a lot of flair and relatively little money. She could put a whole room together with just a few bits of silk, a bunch of ostrich feathers and a splash of paint."

Built in the 1170s by Adam de Hereford, one of the band of Norman knights who invaded Ireland to claim the land for Henry II, Leixlip Castle has been occupied more or less continuously for eight hundred years. Its location on a rock between the River Liffey and one of its tributaries, the Rye Water, about 32 kilometres (20 miles) from Dublin, has been its salvation. Because it was close to the seat of English power in Dublin, the castle escaped most of the conflicts and depredations afflicting castles further afield through centuries of conquest and rebellion, famine and civil war.

ROMANTIC
ELEGANCE

BERKELEY FOREST

OPPOSITE: *The painted wood floor in the guest bedroom is typical of the Scandinavian influence of Berkeley Forest's Danish-born owner. Painted chequered floors are common in Denmark. The emerald green of the walls in the guest bedroom is echoed in the crowns and Celtic motifs stencilled on to the bedspread.*

LEFT: *The ochre-washed house with its unadorned Georgian windows and simple Doric portico is typical of many medium-size Irish country houses. The parkland is home to a flock of Suffolk Cross sheep nurtured by Gunnar Bernstorff. On the slope behind the house, from where the Blackstairs Mountains are visible, the Bernstorffs have created a wonderful garden.*

IN HIS BOOK *THE QUERIST,* GEORGE BERKELEY, the early eighteenth-century philosopher and Church of Ireland bishop, wondered whether "any people in Europe were so meanly provided with houses and furniture in proportion to their incomes" as the Anglo–Irish gentry. The economic disruption caused by the Williamite wars, the paucity of skilled builders and craftsmen and the cost of transporting and shipping imported goods all contributed to the less luxurious living standards enjoyed by settlers in Ireland compared with their English cousins. Irish fiction, ranging from the novels of Maria Edgeworth to those of Molly Keane, furnishes numerous examples of the "poor-relation syndrome" and the often desperate strategies resorted to by the Anglo–Irish to keep up appearances in the face of the real or imagined slights from the more affluent English. Snobberies of title and rank and the habit of advertising one's famous connections persisted in Ireland long after they had ceased to be socially acceptable across the water.

Berkeley Forest, one of the more charming of the smaller Georgian country houses to have survived, epitomizes the Anglo–Irish tendency to drop famous names. Its connection with the Berkeley family, including its most illustrious member, George Berkeley, is tenuous to say the least. The present house, dating from the late eighteenth century, incorporates a smaller residence built around 1690 on a beautiful site in gently rolling countryside looking towards the distant Blackstairs Mountains near New Ross, County Wexford. Its refurbisher was Colonel Joseph Deane, who inherited the estate

OPPOSITE: *A Victorian wicker phaeton and an early perambulator made by a local carriage-maker take pride of place in the old dining room, housing the antique toy collection.* BELOW: *Ghostly figures in crinolines and bustles hover in the upstairs saloon, now home to a collection of eighteenth-century period costumes.*

from his cousin Colonel Berkeley, who in turn was distantly related to the famous philosopher–bishop. As well as stressing the family connection, Deane wanted the house to reflect his newly dignified status as a member of the Irish Parliament. (George Berkeley, despite the brilliance of his mind, was not above such snobbery himself, rejoicing in his own connection, through a junior branch of the family, to the great Earls of Berkeley in England.)

Like so many Irish country houses, great and small, Berkeley Forest saw a decline in its fortunes, losing most of its original furniture and suffering from the occupancy of a succession of tenants. It was rescued thirty years ago by Danish-born Count Gunnar Bernstorff and his wife, Irish designer and artist Anne Griffin. The Bernstorffs have given the house a remarkably bright and uncluttered look, with a strong Scandinavian flavour. Instead of the Turkish carpets, mahogany sideboards and four-poster beds typical of the middle-sized Irish country house, there are painted floors and bedsteads furnished with bright-coloured quilts in clean modern designs. The *pièce-de-résistance* is the small family museum, open to the public, housing a unique collection of antique dolls and toys and period costumes. Anne had to make diminutive padded wire models to fit the much smaller size of our eighteenth-century ancestors.

BANTRY HOUSE

ABOVE: *Bantry House occupies a commanding position over Bantry Bay in west Cork,
looking towards the Caha Mountains on the Beara Peninsula. The fortunes of its owners
rose with the failure of the attempted invasion by the French in 1796.*
OPPOSITE: *Over 18 metres (60 feet) long, the library with its splendid marble columns
brings the two wings of Bantry House together. It was added by the second Earl of
Bantry in the 1850s.*

I F THERE IS A SINGLE PROPERTY THAT EPITOMIZES the Anglo–Irish country
house, both in its past glory and in its more recent decline and revival, it must
be Bantry House in County Cork. With its air of fading yet overblown
opulence, its spectacular setting on Bantry Bay and the intimate connection
between its family's fortunes and that of the nation, it gathers to itself the spirit
of history as effortlessly as the muses that grace its lawns.

The present owner, Egerton Shelswell-White, inherited Bantry from his mother,
Clodagh, a descendant of the Earls of Bantry, in 1978. The task his mother and he faced
was a formidable one. Both wings of the house were condemned as unsafe. There was dry
rot and rising damp, and the enormous weight of the lead on the roof had caused the walls
to buckle dangerously. To pay for the repairs, Clodagh sold the remaining land. Helped
by his wife, Brigitte, and their six children, Egerton is now completing Clodagh's project.

ABOVE: *Spanish brass and bronzes adorn a massive gilded sideboard made specially for the dining room.*

LEFT: *The dining room, where guests were entertained beneath the regal gaze of King George III and Queen Charlotte. The still-life above the fireplace is attributed to the seventeenth-century Flemish painter Frans Snyders.*

57

ABOVE: *Marble busts of
members of the White
family flank the entrance
to the inner hall. A
nineteenth-century Dutch
overmantel rests above the
mantelpiece.*

RIGHT: *In the ante-room
Piranesi prints showing
scenes of classical Rome
hang on the original
Victorian wallpaper. The
hall chairs were made
locally, from holly. The
nineteenth-century
mantelpiece was designed
by the Victorian painter
Angelica Kauffmann.*

A keen performer on the bass trombone – he is co-founder of the Bantry Band – he devotes his considerable energy to restoring the house. The wings have been turned into comfortable bed-and-breakfast accommodation, while the staterooms and grounds now receive nearly fifty thousand visitors a year.

Bantry House was built by the Hutchinson family *c*1710, when it was known as Blackrock. A decade later it was purchased by Councillor Richard White, whose family had been settled in the area since the seventeenth century. As White continued to prosper, he acquired most of the surrounding land. His grandson, also Richard, converted his modest fortune into spectacular success for his family, by a combination of good luck and cool thinking during a momentous incident in 1796. The circumstances were these: In December an army of sixteen thousand under the command of the French General Hoche set sail from France in a fleet of forty-three ships. On board was a Dublin Protestant lawyer named Wolfe Tone who had induced the French to attempt an invasion of Ireland. Tone's plan was to overthrow the monarchist government with the help of the French Republic by coordinating an Irish rebellion with the invasion. The United Irishmen, a secret revolutionary brotherhood he had founded, would help to lead the uprising. However, events did not go as planned. Devastated by ferocious gales, most of the ships were forced to turn back, and only sixteen reached Bantry Bay, with six thousand men. Neither Tone nor Hoche was among them. Richard White summoned help from Cork, which arrived in the shape of a scanty four hundred British redcoats.

ABOVE: *Detail of the outer hall: the portrait above the table is Egerton Shelswell-White's great-grandmother, Lady Elizabeth White, daughter of the third Earl of Bantry.*

ABOVE LEFT: *The chequered floor of the inner hall, which contains a collection of travelling and storage chests, is part of the original eighteenth-century house.*

RIGHT: *A nineteenth-century portrait of Gladys Herbert, a cousin of the White family, as a little girl is reflected in a gilt mirror on the main staircase. She died soon after the picture was painted. The first and second flights of stairs date from the original house. The upper flights were added as part of the nineteenth-century alterations.*

ABOVE: *A pair of marble busts of the second Earl of Bantry and his wife, Mary O'Brien, a descendant of Brian Boru, last High King of Ireland, by the Irish sculptor Richard Hogan, c1830, in Bantry's outer hall.*

A local man was sent to sell victuals to one of the ships. When asked by the French how many troops were on shore he replied, "Twenty thousand," adding that a British fleet was just around the Cape. Leaderless, seasick and thoroughly demoralized, the would-be invaders sailed back to France.

Richard White's presence of mind earned him a peerage. As Baron Bantry he was able to marry into the aristocracy, and he was promoted to Earl in 1816. His son, Viscount Berehaven, sent back shiploads of furniture from his Grand Tour of Europe. Despite the addition in 1820 of a six-bay central block with two drawing rooms and bedrooms above, facing north across the sea, the house was too small to accommodate the collection of furniture. In 1845 Viscount Berehaven remodelled the house and grounds, adding two more wings facing south towards the hill, on which he planted trees and laid out terraces. The house, constructed over at least four different periods, was given the appearance of

unity by the stone balustrade surrounding the roof and the giant brick pilasters and brick window surrounds that enliven the façade, making a pleasing contrast to the walls of rough grey stone.

In 1891 the fourth and last Earl of Bantry died without male heirs and the title became extinct. The property passed through a succession of female heirs to its present owner. During the Irish Civil War, when the only hospital in Bantry was burned down, the family offered the house as a temporary hospital. During the Second World War the Irish Army was billeted in the grounds, the stables and part of the house. Even in neutral Ireland, Bantry retained its strategic location. By 1946 when Bantry became the first stately home south of the border to open its doors to the public, history had come full circle. A magnificent stately home built on the ruined hopes of the United Irishmen survived for the benefit of all the people of Ireland.

ABOVE: *A nineteenth-century travelling shrine hung with fifteenth- and sixteenth-century icons brought back from Russia by the second Earl stands in the inner hall. Such family icons were carried on horseback when their owners moved from city to country dwellings.*

ROMANTIC
ELEGANCE

CASTLE LESLIE

ABOVE: *The family's Irish fortunes were founded in the seventeenth century by Bishop John Leslie. The original estate comprised 12,000 hectares (30,000 acres), but under the 1903 Wyndham Land Act the land was redistributed to tenants by the Land Commission. Today Castle Leslie retains only the 400 hectares (1,000 acres) that are enclosed within the demesne wall.*
OPPOSITE: *A panel throne presides beneath a portrait of a Spanish infanta against the end wall of the drawing room.*

CASTLE LESLIE, AT GLASLOUGH IN COUNTY MONAGHAN, is probably the last great house in Ireland conceived for pleasure and entertainment. It seems thoroughly appropriate that this function has been restored in its new incarnation as a country house hotel. The present house was built for Sir John Leslie, MP, the first Baronet, *c*1870; the Leslie family had lived on the site since the mid-seventeenth century. Inspired by his travels, Sir John determined to build an Italianate villa overlooking the lake for himself and his young wife. He ill-advisedly went away during the construction and on his return was horrified to find that his Ulster architects had provided him with a dour grey stone pile in the Scots baronial style – an object lesson, if ever one was needed, on the perils of absenteeism. Nevertheless there remains of his original desire a charming Renaissance-style annex modelled on Michelangelo's cloister

LEFT: *The fourteen bedrooms all have en-suite bathrooms decorated by Sir John (Jack) Leslie's niece. The initials "J" and "C" carved on the mantelpiece are those of John and Constance, the first Baronet and his wife.*

BELOW: *The blue bedroom. The portrait is of Sir Shane's sister-in-law, Ann Cochrane, wife of the Irish–American Congressman, Bourke Cochrane, who is said to have taught Winston Churchill the art of oratory.*

LEFT: *The bathroom of the nursery bedroom is contained within the walls of a giant dolls' house. Once the Leslie children's schoolroom, the nursery was "the focal point of much family emotion" according to Sir John's nephew, Tarka. The old dolls' house – now in England – provided the inspiration for Samantha's unusual creation.*

65

ABOVE: *The mauve bedroom is one of many available to paying guests at Castle Leslie. On the mantelpiece is a Louis XVI clock, and above hangs a late eighteenth-century Irish Chippendale mirror. The eighteenth-century prints on either side of the fireplace are French.*

at Santa Maria degli Angeli in Rome. And the interior of the main house has a warm Renaissance flavour which goes a considerable way towards compensating for the cold, gabled exterior.

Sir John's talent as an artist is revealed in a series of frescoes he painted behind the cloister. While serving in the Life Guards he had the distinction of exhibiting a painting in the Royal Academy the same year as he won the Grand Military Steeplechase. However, it was during the tenure of his son that Castle Leslie fully came into its own.

The second Baronet – also Sir John – married Leonie, one of three beautiful daughters of Leonard Jerome of New York. Her sister Jennie married Lord Randolph Churchill. The house was frequented by the most fashionable Edwardian society, including Queen Margaret of Sweden, the Duke of Connaught (Queen Victoria's youngest son) and Prince Pierre de Monaco (Prince Rainier's father), and the young Winston sometimes visited his

uncle and aunt. Just as well that Castle Leslie boasted the first-ever gas stove and plumbed bathroom in Ireland and that a huge boiler had been installed to heat the reception rooms. There was even a hand-operated elevator to take visitors' luggage upstairs.

The Leslies are known for both their mild eccentricity and their distinctive literary bent. The early eighteenth-century Anglo–Irish satirist Jonathan Swift, a regular visitor to the earlier castle that was on this site, wrote of "Glaslough with rows of books upon its shelves/written by Leslies all about themselves". The tradition has continued to the present. The third Baronet, Sir Shane Leslie, is best known for his ghost stories; but he was also a poet and (unlike his father) an ardent Irish nationalist who converted to Roman Catholicism. He renounced his inheritance and retreated to a monastery with the intention of entering the priesthood. However, to the delight of his Protestant family, he soon abandoned his vocation to marry an American beauty, Marjorie Ide of Vermont.

ABOVE: *In the blue bedroom an early eighteenth-century firescreen stands in front of the marble mantelpiece, brought from the old house. Round tinted prints after Morland hang on either side of an Italian gilt mirror. The clock is dated 1830 and is probably French.*

ROMANTIC
ELEGANCE

CASTLE LESLIE

LEFT: *The cabinets in the drawing room contain a collection of Leslie campaign medals and, behind, a portrait by the first Baronet of his daughter Docia, aged sixteen. The pair of glass candelabra and the classical architectural models came from Stratford Place, the Leslie family house in London.*

RIGHT: *A copy of Jacopo da Bassano's* Flight into Egypt *hangs above the della Robbia mantelpiece of glazed terracotta in the drawing room. The black Wedgwood cameos are still inscribed with the 1777 price of ten shillings and sixpence. On the table to the left of the fireplace are two painted miniatures of Anita and Sir John (Jack) Leslie.*

BELOW: *An eighteenth-century painting depicting scenes from a chase at a Hapsburg hunting lodge hangs in the grand hall above a sixteenth-century Spanish* vargueño, *which was used by monks as a kind of filing cabinet.*

ABOVE: *The Chinese bedroom has been restored to its original colour. The shutters are decorated with gilt bamboo motifs and the walls have a painted frieze. The green painted cupboard has decorated red panels with a wallpaper base. The curtains are of gold brocade.*

He stood as the Nationalist candidate for Londonderry in the 1910 General Election, losing by only fifty-nine votes to the Unionist candidate, the Duke of Abercorn. Sir Shane's religious and political allegiance may well have saved Castle Leslie from being burned down during the "Troubles" after the First World War. After his younger brother was killed in action in 1914 the estate was made over to Sir Shane's son, John Norman (Jack) Leslie, who in due course became the fourth and present Baronet.

Until recently, Sir John lived in Rome, and the castle and estate were managed by his sister, the author Anita Leslie, who has since died, and their younger brother, Desmond. During the 1950s Desmond claimed to have had a close encounter with extra-terrestrials when, it is said, a flying saucer landed on the lake: the result was *Flying Saucers Have Landed,* a best-seller written with George Adamski. Desmond currently lives in France. The hotel is run by Desmond's daughter, Samantha, and her husband, Ultan Bannon.

The transformation of Castle Leslie into a hotel has not spoiled the sense of continuity with the past. The rooms are still filled with Italian and Spanish artefacts brought home by Leslies, along with other mementoes from their travels. Leslie ancestors still look down from the walls. The family feeling is consummated by the comings and goings of various living Leslies – including Sir John and his nephew Tarka, who are happy to amuse guests with anecdotes about their ancestors.

For example, the family motto "Grip Fast" was coined by Margaret Tudor, Queen of Scotland, after she was heroically rescued from a river by a galloping Leslie while fleeing from her enemies; and there are stories about Dean Charles Leslie, the "choleric cleric" who inspired Dr Johnson to remark, "Leslie is a reasoner against whom it is difficult to reason." A stay at Castle Leslie is a history lesson that slips down as effortlessly as drinks by the fire in the elegant Italianate drawing room.

ABOVE: *The green bedroom belonged to the second Baronet and has not been changed since the house was built. On the Victorian chest of drawers stands a bronze statue of Queen Victoria's third son, the five-year-old Prince Arthur (Duke of Connaught) holding the state sword of the Duke of Wellington, his godfather.*

DISORDER

THE OLD SCHOOL

OPPOSITE: *When Phillipa Bayliss and her former husband bought the Old School there were no inside stairs so they made this spiral staircase leading to the upper-floor schoolroom. The portrait is of Phillipa's grandfather and the painted wooden figures are part of an installation based on Monteverdi's opera* Orfeo, *which she exhibited in London.*

LEFT: *The Old School overlooking the Grand Canal. Most of the small rural National Schools were provided with a stone plaque on which was carved the name and sometimes the date of the building. This one, set above the classical porch, is carved in both English and Gaelic.*

WHEN PAINTER PHILLIPA BAYLISS bought the Old School in 1971 with her then husband, William Garner, it had been used to store hay for more than twenty years. The Old School had been closed in 1949 to make way for the new school by the canal bridge nearer the main road. The schoolhouse was a bargain for the couple, who had three sons to feed and little cash to spare. The canal-side plot next to the house allowed Phillipa to create a secret garden of roses and borders of wild flowers, which has proved a constant source of inspiration for her paintings – a miniature Giverny in the tranquil Kildare countryside less than half an hour from Dublin.

The Old School was built in 1810 by Lord Cloncurry, who, like many of the big landowners of the time, was keen to demonstrate his desire to improve the lot of the common people in his area. It was intended for the children of the growing workforce involved in the building of the Grand Canal, which bordered one side of Lord Cloncurry's demesne. Lord Cloncurry himself built a private canal station on his Lyons House estate nearby, featuring a range of handsome Georgian buildings. The Old School is mentioned in *Lewis's Topography* (published in 1829) as having ninety pupils. In 1839 it was turned into a National School under the system established to provide schooling for Roman Catholic children, especially the poor, after the penal laws which forced Catholics to send their children to the notorious Hedge Schools fell into disuse.

SWEET
DISORDER

THE OLD SCHOOL

RIGHT: *The view from the studio into Phillipa's garden provides a constant source of subject matter.* BELOW AND OPPOSITE: *The bed in Phillipa's bedroom belonged to her American great-grandmother. The quilted bedspread echoes her painting of flowers that hangs above it.*

ABOVE: *Phillipa chose the colours in the main living room to counteract the grey winter light. The blue curtains, when drawn, resemble the sky. She based the design of the needlepoint chair to the right of the table on a Vasarely print. The hanging-basket lights, which are made of shower curtain and fake greenery, "disguise those terrible long-life, low-energy bulbs".*

The first canal in Ireland was built in 1731. By the last quarter of the eighteenth century, canal construction had reached fever pitch, with the Grand Canal and the Royal Canal competing to connect Dublin harbour to the River Shannon. As writer Brendan Lehane explains, "It seems an absurd extravagance that two canals, enormous ventures, should co-exist in a land never noted for prosperity, but the enthusiasm for building canals in George III's reign was like the acquisition of airlines by semi-bankrupt states in our own day." As well as commercial traffic the canals could have provided cheap transport for passengers, had the companies building them not lavished money (thirty thousand pounds in the case of the Grand Canal) on hotels that could never hope to be full. The Grand Canal's heyday was during the first half of the nineteenth century, when hotels, warehouses and other canal architecture sprang up to service the growing demand. But then the railways arrived, undermining the waterways, and the Great Famine destroyed the Irish economy. Nevertheless, the canals continued to be used for commercial transport until the late 1950s.

Lord Cloncurry was well known for his liberal tendencies. He was imprisoned by William Pitt the Younger in the Tower of London for two years without trial, for his advanced political views and friendship with some of the United Irishmen (whose avowed aim was to overthrow the British in Ireland). But, though a patriot, when it came to aesthetics he eschewed Hibernian references and employed the architect Richard Morrison to make changes of a severe neoclassical nature to the colonnades and wings of

LEFT: *Phillipa painted all
the furniture in the
schoolroom, including the
corner cupboard with its
elegant glass doors.*
TOP: *The Waterford stove
at the kitchen end of the
room displays two still-lifes
by Phillipa.*
ABOVE: *A console
embellished by Phillipa
supports an eclectic display
of ornaments.*

79

RIGHT: *A detail of Phillipa's handiwork in the bathroom showing a giant water lily under the window and bamboos in the corner of the bath. It took her only two days to decorate the entire room – walls, ceiling, washing machine and floor.*

ABOVE AND OPPOSITE: *An Irish milking stool painted red complements the greens in the mural Phillipa painted in the bathroom in response to a suggestion by one of her sons. "I had to think of a way of disguising the exposed pipe and the general decrepitude, so a jungly glade seemed logical," she says.*

Lyons House. Perhaps this accounts for the little classical porch with fluted Doric columns and triglyphs at the Old School – a most unusual feature in school architecture. Eventually Lord Cloncurry's passion for classical artefacts led to disaster when a large shipment of Italian antiquities he had purchased was wrecked off Wicklow Head. To this day His Lordship's marbles lie at the bottom of the sea.

Since William and Phillipa have parted company and their three sons have grown up, the Old School has remained Phillipa's home. She spends her time painting in the ground-floor studio or the garden and occasionally giving lessons. After the heat and bustle of travel, the Old School is an oasis of calm and hospitality. Children and grandchildren gravitate there, along with ambassadors, artists, writers and other members of Phillipa's eclectic band of friends. When the guests have departed, there remains the life of the canal: the splutterings of ducks and moorhens, the lazy flow of the waters and the play of its reflections on the ceiling.

SWEET
DISORDER

BALLINTERRY

OPPOSITE: *Bohemian glass candelabras and a Chinoiserie mirror set against the dull green walls of the drawing room reflect the evening sun. A wooden horse from a Mexican carousel raises its head above a sea of red geraniums. "Every Irish house must have its horse," says the owner, Hurd Hatfield.*

LEFT: *A listed (registered) ancient monument, Ballinterry dates from the thirteenth century. Having long survived the turbulent history of Ireland, it was about to have its roof removed when Hurd found it while staying nearby in 1974. The small scale of the house, with its simple Queen Anne front, is unusual in Ireland.*

HURD HATFIELD IS ONE OF THOSE GIFTED Americans whose childhood imaginations become so enthralled by some obscure detail of European culture that sooner or later they find themselves compelled to make a creative response. They are a rare species whose resources of energy, determination and creativity are truly enviable.

Although best known as an actor, famously for the title role in the 1936 film version of Oscar Wilde's *The Picture of Dorian Gray*, Hurd's other passion is old houses. As a child he spent his family holidays in a converted old tavern in New Jersey and fell under the spell of the eighteenth century without even knowing what it was. It was this that set him off on a series of love affairs with various old houses (seven in all), culminating with the purchase in 1974 of Ballinterry – his first Irish house and the ultimate love of his life. At the time Hurd was visiting the American actress Angela Lansbury, who lived in another period house nearby. He fell in love with Ballinterry at first sight, saving it from possible demolition by its owners, who found it too large and had already deserted it for a cottage on the land.

Ballinterry, in County Cork, is one of the oldest continuously inhabited houses in Ireland. Parts of it date from the thirteenth century. The medieval towers in the grounds suggest a fortified dwelling, some of which was incorporated into the present house. The Queen Anne front is dramatically different from the back, which has a patchwork of

ABOVE: *Two eighteenth-century Chinese plates, with the sacred bird and butterfly design, hang on ribbons against red panelling. The colour scheme was inspired by Hurd's recent trip to Russia.*

LEFT: *The music room was created after a fire. On the table stands a photograph of George V with his doomed cousin Nicholas II of Russia. The table setting, with name cards for the nineteenth-century French novelist George Sand and her friends, was inspired by Sand's studio in Nohant, France.*

85

BELOW: *The blue library,
with bookcases from a
demolished eighteenth-
century shop. An Irish
birthing chair stands below
a portrait of Hurd's father.*
OPPOSITE: *A detail of the
green drawing room
showing the candelabra
mirror and, on the right,
a sculpture of Hurd by
the German artist
Margarita Garthe.*

ancient stones with half-revealed arches and filled-in windows, charting the house's evolution over the centuries.

But behind the discreet façade of Ballinterry there exists a richly imaginative and creative world quite at odds with its unpretentious exterior. The mood of the rooms – each one dramatically different from the next – is created by juxtaposing all sorts of objects from different eras and parts of the world. In 1991 a fire burnt down the north side of the house and many objects were lost. Hurd's response was typical. Undaunted by the disaster and full of ideas, he threw himself into schemes for renovation. All the new rooms have a theatrical aspect, but none more so than the music room, created after the fire and inspired by Hurd's association with Russia through his old friend and mentor Mikhail Chekhov, "the giant of Russian theatre".

All the threads of Hurd's long and varied life are woven together with the soul of the house, as if each needed the other in order to flourish: America (he is a New Yorker), Ireland, his love of Europe and India, his acting and dancing life, his artistic and reading life, and his love for his friends, both living and dead. The interior design is of the sensitive, understated variety, and he uses colour to create a sense of mystery, "to show the wash of time over things".

THE BIRDMEN OF MULLET

ABOVE: *A pair of papier-mâché swans standing on columns made from whitewashed tar barrels guards the entrance to Pine Cottage. Other birds and animals made by Anthony Coyle for his garden menagerie include a pied cow and an ostrich. The Coyles have lived together since their mother died more than forty years ago.*
OPPOSITE: *In the kitchen, cabinets display a variety of wildlife, principally birds, that are native to the area.*

THE MULLET PENINSULA, WHICH JUTS INTO THE ATLANTIC off the coast of County Mayo, is one of the poorest and least-known parts of the West of Ireland. A low-lying, treeless region of small farms, sand dunes and bogland, it has no celebrated lakes or mountains nor salmon-crowded rivers with which to entice the visitor. Its charms are more esoteric – the flights of dunlins and oyster-catchers, the cry of the curlew in the wind, the immensity of the sky . . . and the bustle of market day when most of the adult population descends on the town of Belmullet to buy and sell and to exchange gossip in the bars.

Created by improving landlords in the eighteenth century, Belmullet has seen better days. In the 1830s it was described as a place "where you could see industry in all its stirring shapes . . . large and well-built stores . . . masts of ships lying at the ends of the

RIGHT: *A life-size statue of the Virgin, painted by Anthony Coyle, presides over the living room where he and his brother, Michael, spend their evenings surrounded by their collection of stuffed and papier-mâché birds. Anthony is a keen disciple of Charles Darwin.*

ABOVE: *A wooden cut-out of a peregrine falcon, crafted and painted by Anthony, casts a beady eye over Anthony's bedroom.*

ABOVE: *With his sheepdog, Cuchulain, named after the Irish mythological hero, Anthony Coyle sits by the fire. The kitchen dresser is exactly as it was when Mother Coyle died.*

OPPOSITE: *Geraniums flank the porch beneath an array of posters depicting an assortment of animals, both domestic and wild. Anthony and Michael added the porch to their cottage in order to prevent unwelcome intruders, such as ducks and sheep, from foraging in their collection of bric-a-brac.*

principal streets". For most of the past century, however, the region has been in decline. The peninsula's inhabitants, like other Mayo folk, have close family connections with England, and several people from Mullet have made fortunes in the construction industry, notably in Birmingham and the West Midlands.

Michael and Anthony Coyle are exceptions. Mulleteers to the last, they have lived in the same three-room bungalow, in the most exposed corner of the peninsula, since their mother died more than forty years ago. Flying in the face of nature, they have protected Pine Cottage with an exotic belt of shrubs and trees – bog willows, lombardy poplars, escallonia, bamboo canes, New Zealand flax and cordyline palms – added to the more familiar windbreaks composed of fuchsia and rhododendron. Born in the village across the bay, the brothers are still regarded as "foreigners", which licenses them to indulge in fantasies denied to other Mullet folk. As a boy Anthony collected birds' eggs – until his mother told him the habit would send him to hell. Now, as if to make amends, he has become a breeder of birds, raising golden pheasants, guinea-fowl and rare breeds of duck in his garden, while keeping an eye on the peregrine falcons that nest on nearby cliffs.

The cottage has become a secret folk museum, with the original collection of eggs (of which, despite his mother's warning, Anthony is immensely proud) supplemented by stuffed fish, animal paintings and silhouettes of birds, all presided over by the benign presence of the Blessed Virgin, "Queen of Ireland".

SWEET
DISORDER

PICKERING FOREST

ABOVE: *When she bought Pickering Forest in 1990, Marina Guinness was the only bidder. As well as good grazing land, the plot includes nearly three hectares (about six acres) of ancient beech wood around the house, described disparagingly by the estate agent as "waste land".*
OPPOSITE: *Marina's stepmother, Penny Guinness, gave her the mirror advertising a rival and less successful brewery. The walls were decorated by the artist Phillipa Bayliss, who lives nearby, at the Old School (qv).*

BUYING PICKERING FOREST, a rambling late eighteenth-century house in County Kildare, was an impulsive act for Marina Guinness. Her mother, Mariga, had recently died, leaving an eclectic array of belongings spread out among different houses in Ireland, England, Scotland and Norway – the residue of a life spent collecting thousands of books and any beautiful object that struck her fancy. Marina urgently needed space to house her burgeoning collection.

Pickering Forest had belonged to the Brooke family, whose last member, Mabel, Lady Brooke, was a well-known local character. "Before a party," according to Henry McDowell, long-time local resident and friend of Marina's, "the first objective was to dry out the carpet, and fires were kept burning night and day while steam gently misted over the chandeliers and mirror glass. When the room filled with people, little droplets of

ABOVE: *The paper frieze in the library was designed by David Skinner, a local craftsman. Originally commissioned for the ceiling of St Aidan's Cathedral, Enniscorthy, it was cut into strips for use here. The yellow paint is coated with a matt glaze mixed with gold paint powder. Above the mantelpiece hangs a print of the Salmon Leap at Leixlip Castle (qv), Marina's parents' home.*

condensation fell unnoticed from the ceiling." It was only after moving into the house that Marina became aware that she had problems of her own. When it rained, water cascaded down the stairs. Then there was the horrible revelation that the baths were emptying into the basement, which had become a fetid underground lake.

But the most devastating discovery was the dry rot, which put many of the floors in serious danger of collapsing. Marina found some solace when her father, Desmond Guinness, explained that although he had known of people being driven to suicide by the cost of repairing dry rot, he was not aware of any deaths caused by falling through a rotting floor. There is also a resident ghost who makes an appalling din at two minutes to five most mornings.

It was to be years before all the structural repairs were completed and the builders were finally banished. Objects still arrive from here and there, as if by magic, to fill empty spaces, and the feeling of the house is warm and inviting. A constant stream of visitors is escorted up and down the pot-holed avenue by a posse of yapping dogs. Having survived the canine gauntlet, the visitor is immediately put at ease. Tea is always brewing on the Aga, food is about to be served and Marina is there to welcome.

ABOVE: *The dining-room walls were painted bright red to "cheer up the gloomy seascapes", says Marina. The zebra head once hung on the wall, but crashed down during a particularly boisterous dinner party, narrowly missing someone's head. "The alligator makes diners nervous and encourages them to eat everything on their plates."*

LEFT: *Marina has only recently completed the daunting task of sorting through her late mother's possessions and distributing them throughout the house. The bed in the green bedroom comes from a Chinese opium den. Unusually long, it was designed to allow two people to lie together while sharing a pipe.*

SWEET
DISORDER

HUNTINGTON CASTLE

OPPOSITE: *A pair of crooked candlesticks pays homage to a portrait of Olivia, the heroine of Shakespeare's* Twelfth Night. *The portrait was painted by William Powell Frith, the Victorian artist made famous by such classic narrative paintings as* Derby Day.

LEFT: *Huntington Castle from the stableyard gates, with nineteenth-century additions. The castle was built on the site of an abbey, and ghostly friars are said to appear at dusk near the old yew walk, one of the oldest in Europe.*

ON ST PATRICK'S DAY 1966, Lawrence Durdin-Robertson, a Church of Ireland clergyman and owner of Huntington Castle in County Carlow, had a mystical experience. While walking up his avenue where ghostly friars are said to glide at dusk, he had a sudden intuition or revelation, which convinced him that God is female. Undaunted by the disapproval of his bishop, not to mention his Anglo–Irish neighbours, he began to publish pamphlets about the Goddess. Together with his sister, Olivia, and his wife, Pamela, he founded the Fellowship of Isis. A hybrid of ecology, feminism, New Age religiosity and eastern spirituality, underpinned by Lawrence's scholarly studies in ancient religions, the fellowship now claims a membership of more than fourteen thousand in over ninety countries.

Lawrence, or "Derry" as he was known, and Pamela have since passed away; but the Fellowship lives on under Olivia, the High Priestess of Isis. Lawrence's son David now owns the castle, which is open to the public between June and August. Everyone who visits is invited to join. Olivia explains the Fellowship's popularity in language that combines modern feminist theology with ancient paganism and ecological concerns: "People feel the feminine element has been pushed out of their religions. Even in Catholic churches they are complaining that statues of Our Lady are being discarded. Recent apparations at Lourdes, Fatima, Knock, Garabondal, Medjugorge and other places all emphasize that the earth is faced with destruction because of the mad, male

RIGHT: *The ground-floor
"gents'" testifies to the
markswomanship of
Nora Parsons, mother of
Olivia and Derry Durdin-
Robertson. She shot the
crocodile in India at the
age of seventeen. The
Goddess would doubtless
have disapproved,
considering Her well-
known hostility to any
blood sports.*

ABOVE: *The High Altar
dedicated to Isis. The
figure of the Goddess was
carved by Derry's son,
David, the castle's
present owner.*
OPPOSITE: *A mother and
child guard the stairs
leading up to the library
where Lawrence "Derry"
Durdin-Robertson
conducted his researches
into the Goddess in Her
previous manifestations.*

misappropriation of God's creative power. The whole world is threatened by a
patriarchal technocracy, with people vivisecting animals, experimenting with germ
warfare, spreading nuclear weapons . . ."

As part of the effort to reverse the headlong rush towards global disaster, the whole of
the basement of Huntingdon Castle has been given over to the Goddess in her myriad
manifestations. She is Hathor the Cow, Sekhet the Lioness, Lakshmi, Demeter, Parvati
and Kali. The kitchens, sculleries and cellars that once serviced the castle have been
transformed into oratories. Cold, bleak cellars where footmen polished and parlour-
maids scrubbed are now aglow with icons, statues, candelabras and trays of offerings.
Even the old kitchen utensils, including a cauldron straight out of the witches' parlour in
Macbeth, are enlisted in the celebration of the Eternal Feminine. The centrepiece is the
High Altar of Isis. Her statue, carved in wood, reveals David Durdin-Robertson's talent

LEFT: *In the dining room generations of Esmondes, Durdins and Robertsons gaze down benignly from their gilt frames on to the collection of family silver displayed on the mahogany sideboard in typical Anglo–Irish fashion. The seventeenth-century fireplace has been cleverly adapted to create a hatch leading straight into the kitchen.*

OPPOSITE: *A nineteenth-century neoclassical statue of* Diana the Huntress, *one of the Goddess's numerous manifestations, reclining on the back of a lion, is the centrepiece of the tapestry room, where family portraits are displayed against the fading grandeur of eighteenth-century tapestries.*

as a sculptor. At solstices and equinoxes and other festivals in the Goddess's calendar, devotees crowd around the High Altar while the Priests and Priestesses of Isis utter chants and prayers not heard in Ireland for the past two thousand years.

The Esmondes, who built Huntington Castle in 1630, had their share of religious troubles. Lord Esmonde was a Protestant, and his Irish Catholic wife, Aylish O'Flaherty, ran off with their infant son, Thomas, fearing he would be raised as a heretic. By the statutes of the time this was enough to have the marriage dissolved and the boy dispossessed.

But while remaining true to his Catholic faith, Thomas Esmonde had the house restored to him after raising a troop of Royalist cavalry during the English Civil War, when the castle was occupied by Cromwellian troops. After the Restoration a grateful Charles II rewarded him with a baronetcy. Thomas's son, Sir Lawrence, was able to

OPPOSITE: *The
conservatory, an
Edwardian addition, is
dominated by a grapevine
that originated as a cutting
from the one at Hampton
Court, near London.*
BELOW: *The tapestry
room was refurbished in
the late nineteenth century,
along with most of the rest
of the house.*

return unchallenged in 1680, and made the castle his family home, bequeathing it to his three daughters, one of whom, Helen, married Richard Durdin.

The castle remained in the Durdin family for more than a century, during which time the library and a small chapel were added. In 1890 the property passed by marriage into the Scottish Robertson family who, as was customary in the case of female inheritance, added the original owners' name to their own. Three generations of Durdin-Robertsons now live in the castle: Olivia; David and his wife, Moira; and David and Moira's children.

Apart from the odd statue, the Goddess is strictly confined to the basement. The upper floors have hardly been touched in the past century – one reason, no doubt, that Stanley Kubrick made it the setting for *Barry Lyndon*, his 1975 film of Thackeray's novel about Anglo–Irish impoverishment and greed. The stairs and passages are dark and gloomy, with heavy wooden panelling and thick woollen carpets. The rooms are cluttered with objects and bric-a-brac acquired by generations of Esmondes, Durdins and Robertsons. Until recently there was an almost complete absence of electric light, and guests often found themselves going to bed by candlelight. Not all is gloom, however: like the sunlit shafts that puncture the soft clouds of rain outside, elegant rooms with fine plaster ceilings dance with reflections, recalling a lost world of gaiety and charm.

SWEET
DISORDER

ORANMORE

ABOVE: *The castle faces due west towards the Atlantic, a tall, stark sentinel against the constant gales and storms. Like other square towers in the area, it was built by Norman settlers in the thirteenth century.*
OPPOSITE: *The main upper room in the keep, once a soldiers' dormitory, is now a large bedroom for the occasional use of guests.*

WHEN THE WRITER ANITA LESLIE, mother of the present owner, Leonie Finn, bought Oranmore in County Galway shortly after the Second World War, it had long been a derelict ruin. The keep with the nearby field cost her less than two hundred pounds. A fortified stronghold built in the thirteenth century, the tower was never exactly comfortable. Anita and her husband, Commander Bill King, failed to conquer the damp. "When we first came," says Bill King, a sprightly nonagenarian, "it actually used to rain indoors. You could stand inside the great hall and see a fine mist gently falling down." The damp has encouraged a profusion of plants to flourish indoors without any assistance from pots or watering cans. Ferns and wild flowers grow quite naturally out of the walls, and can be seen in the crevices under the arrow slits. In one of the small vaulted rooms occasionally used for

SWEET
DISORDER

ORANMORE

RIGHT: *A window in the great hall reveals the massive thickness of the walls. A madonna and two carved wooden chests preserve the medieval atmosphere.*

BELOW: *Festooned with plants and shrubs, this window in the passageway connecting the medieval keep with the modern living quarters shows how skilfully local masons have blended old and new stone.*

LEFT: *The great hall is
furnished in a style that
evokes the castle's
Norman–Gaelic origins.
The Normans rapidly
became "more Irish than
the Irish themselves",
adopting clannish customs
of their own. The castle
last saw military action
during Cromwell's brutal
and bloody Irish campaign
in the mid-seventeenth
century. Fortunately, the
English artillery left the
walls intact.*

guests, the whole window area has become an exotic palm house, with several species of fern nurtured by what looks like centuries of greenish water seeping down the walls.

Leonie, her husband Alec Finn, and their children now live in somewhat drier comfort, in the new dwelling Anita and Bill constructed next to the keep. Anita died several years ago, but Bill still makes regular visits. The fine granite stones used for the new home, which exactly match those of the castle, came from the local Protestant church. Anita happened to be passing while workmen were demolishing it and crushing the handsome cut-stone for road-filler. After bargaining with the foreman, she bought the stones for two shillings and sixpence (twelve and a half pence in today's currency) each. The keep is strictly for guests. "It's a perfect place for parties," says Alec, a successful musician. "You can make a great blaze in the hall. The chimney is so well constructed that it never smokes, even in a gale."

THE PASTORAL

VERSIONS OF
THE PASTORAL

THE MELLON COTTAGE

ABOVE: *The cottage at Camp Hill where Thomas Mellon, founder of the
Mellon family fortunes, was born in 1813.*
OPPOSITE: *View from the kitchen through to the parlour. Originally there were two
rooms – a kitchen and a bedroom. This was spacious compared with the one-room
dwellings many County Tyrone farmers had to share with their animals. In his
autobiography Thomas Mellon described his family as "comfortably fixed".*

THE EPIC OF IRISH EMIGRATION TO AMERICA, with thousands risking
their lives in the fetid squalor of the notorious "Coffin Ships" as a
result of eviction and famine, is so etched into the psyches of Catholic
Ireland and Irish America that a scarcely smaller tide of emigrants, that
of the Ulster Protestants of Scottish descent, is often overlooked.
Yet the contributions made by the Scotch–Irish towards America's
achievements are far from insignificant. There were nine men of Ulster birth or descent
among the fifty-six who signed the Declaration of Independence, and subsequently at
least ten men of Scotch–Irish descent served as president of the United States.

In Ireland dissenters and Presbyterians suffered discrimination along with Catholics,
and took a leading part in the 1798 rebellion inspired by the American colonists' War of
Independence two decades before. (The rebellion, spearheaded by the United Irishmen,

RIGHT: *Detail of the kitchen. A butter-churn stands under the kitchen table with an assortment of bowls and food containers and a milk jug. Traditional kitchen utensils included piggins and noggins, light wooden receptacles used for collecting milk from the cow and buttermilk at churning.*

RIGHT: *The kitchen dresser with its "fiddle front" holds an assortment of dishes and platters. Underneath the lower shelf there are iron cooking pots and cream crocks in which milk still warm from the cow was cooled. A knife-box on the left keeps cutlery out of children's reach.*

FAR RIGHT: *A photo of Thomas Mellon hangs to the right of the hearth, which was the centre of both heating and cooking. The pots could be swung out for easy removal. The bench under the window converts into a double bed. Dual-purpose furniture was commonly used in small cottages. The sword, found during renovations in 1968, is an authentic Mellon heirloom.*

ABOVE: *The main bedroom with its cast-iron bedstead, simple rustic quilt, and Willow Pattern pitcher on the washstand. Some of the items on display in the Mellon Cottage are family heirlooms, but most have been acquired locally to give the rooms an authentic nineteenth-century feel.*

under the leadership of Wolfe Tone, was crushed.) Rural Ulster Protestants were often as poor as their Catholic compatriots and subject to the same afflictions.

By the early nineteenth century, Ireland had become the most densely populated country in Europe, and Ulster was the most densely populated part of Ireland, not least because of the custom of subdividing the land to provide livings for family members. Between 1815 and 1851 about half a million people left Ulster, most for the New World.

The emigrants included members of a particular family whose name became synonymous with wealth and patronage of the arts. Archibald Mellon, whose forebears had settled in Ulster in the 1660s, was a farmer of modest means. Although certainly not poor by the standards of the time, he knew that the family farm, at Camp Hill outside Omagh in County Tyrone, would be too small to support his nine children. He therefore emigrated to America, settling in Pennsylvania in 1816.

His son Andrew was left in charge of the family farm at Camp Hill. Although Andrew, with only one child, Thomas, could easily have supported his family at home, the pull of America and family affection proved too great. In 1818, when Thomas was six, Andrew sold the lease of his farm, including the simple but comfortable cottage he had built for himself between 1816 and 1818, for the sum of two hundred golden guineas (two hundred and ten pounds) and sailed for the United States. The coins were stitched into a belt which his wife fastened around her waist.

In Pennsylvania, after the inevitable hardships, the family prospered. Inspired by Benjamin Franklin's autobiography, young Thomas became a lawyer and then a judge, amassing a fortune in real estate along the way. In 1870 he founded the bank which the next generation of Mellons would transform into one of the most powerful financial institutions in America.

Back in Ireland the cottage at Camp Hill fell into disrepair. By the 1950s it had been reduced to a storehouse and stable, its thatched roof replaced by corrugated iron. Matthew Mellon, assisted by a Northern Ireland government programme of restoration, rallied the family, and the restored cottage became the nucleus of the Ulster American Folk Park, an outdoor museum illustrating the experience of Ulster emigrants. As well as other period cottages from Ulster, the museum has several wooden houses transplanted from America, including an exact replica of the clapboard house Andrew and Thomas built in Pennsylvania.

ABOVE: *The small bedroom with its nineteenth-century iron bed and a child's cradle similar to one in which the infant Thomas Mellon would have slept. When the cottage was restored it was decided to retain the bedrooms and partitions that were added after the Mellons had emigrated.*

117

VERSIONS OF
THE PASTORAL

BOTHAR BUI

OPPOSITE: *The sitting-room end of the stone cabin at Bothar Bui. Hand-woven Irish wool rugs are thrown over the settle – a traditional Irish bench found in cottages and farmhouses. Above it hangs a William Scott lithograph,* Blue Still Life, *echoed on the left wall by a fish frying pan and a griddle-pan for cooking bread.*

LEFT: *The original stone cabin, now the kitchen, dining and living room. The small building on the right is the outbuilding that was turned into an oratory, or abbot's cell, where the more ascetic of the Walkers' friends sometimes sleep. The ancient oak wood descends to the sea, and on the far side of Kenmare Bay MacGillycuddy's Reeks are clearly visible.*

Hazel stealth. A trickle in the culvert.
Athletic sealight on the doorstep slab,
On the sea itself, on silent roofs and gables.

Whitewashed suntraps. Hedges hot as chimneys,
Chairs on all fours. A plate-rack braced and laden.
The fossil poetry of hob and slate.

Desire within its moat, dozing at ease –
Like a gorged cormorant on the rock at noon,
Exiled and in tune with the big glitter.

Re-enter this as the adult of solitude;
The silence-forder and the definite
Presence you sensed withdrawing first time round.
From Seamus Heaney, *Seeing Things* (Faber, 1991)

WHEN DOROTHY AND ROBIN WALKER BEGAN LOOKING for a retreat in southwestern Ireland, they already knew and loved the Beara Peninsula, which is much more rugged and lonely than County Kerry's other, better-known peninsulas, and just as beautiful.

Named after Beara, wife of Owen More, King of Munster during the second century A.D., the peninsula is divided between the counties of Kerry and Cork.

The place the Walkers found was Bothar Bui ("Yellow Lane"), on the border between the two counties. As long ago as 1838, it was marked as a ruin on the Ordnance Survey map. All that remained were two gables from a simple stone cabin. The roof had long gone, trees and shrubs were growing on the inside and most of the walls were broken down. Fortunately, the local builder was a trained stonemason, and he rebuilt the house impeccably, incorporating such local materials as the fine slate slabs used for paving the floors and the ground surrounding the house. The Walkers also restored two small outbuildings – one to serve as a laundry and boilerhouse, and the other as a small oratory or abbott's cell, like those used by the early Christian hermits who settled these shores to seek God in the highlights over the mountains and the play of wind on the sea. Three new buildings were designed by Robin, a practising architect until his death a few years ago. They are discreetly modern in style, with plate-glass fenestration commanding magnificent views across the Bay of Kenmare to the Iveragh Peninsula and MacGillycuddy's Reeks, the highest range of mountains in Ireland. Falling dramatically down the slope between Bothar Bui and the sea lies an ancient oak wood, one of few surviving relics of the forests that covered much of the country in pre-Elizabethan times – before the wars and plantations, and the demands of shipping and agriculture, caused their destruction.

Dorothy's daughter, Sarah, has been living and painting in Bothar Bui since the early 1990s. Dorothy now lives in Dublin but is a frequent visitor. Seamus Heaney, an old friend of the Walkers, is another regular visitor, and the opening poem was inspired by Bothar Bui. Sarah is married to fisherman Kieran Lyons and they have a small son, also Seamus. Kieran works hard beginning in September when the shrimping season starts, and from October until the spring he harvests shrimps and mussels on alternate days, weather permitting. Then follows a respite from the sea, usually taken up with putting right the havoc in the vegetable patch caused by winter storms. In good spring weather the inshore fishermen go after white fish of all varieties. In summer there are crabs and lobsters which flourish in the warm Gulf Stream currents that flow into the inlets. There are also several mussel farms in the bay. Most of the fish are destined for French tables – maintaining the long Irish tradition of exporting fish in preference to eating it at home.

VERSIONS OF
THE PASTORAL

BALLYNABROCKY

ABOVE: *The conservatory designed and built by Ballynabrocky's owner, Patrick Scott,*
blends comfortably with the cut-stone wall of the long barn. "I make a point of
not getting involved in gardening," he says, "as it could develop
into a full-time passion."
OPPOSITE: *A view from the old kitchen, now a sitting room, through the new kitchen to*
the long barn, which doubles as a dining room and studio.

THE FIRST THING PATRICK SCOTT SAW on the day he found Ballynabrocky during the cruel, hard winter of 1963 was a sheep staring out of an upstairs window. The house lay near the end of a road which eventually disappeared into a mountain bog in the Wicklow Hills. It had been empty for more than two years, and its current owner was only interested in a sandpit that lay on the property. A sudden thaw after ten weeks of snow had exposed bodies of many of the sheep that had perished for lack of food when the road was closed. The canny survivors had taken refuge in the cottage. Patrick found the owner at work in his sandpit, and he took the house off his hands for a modest two hundred pounds.

Ballynabrocky, which comes from a Gaelic word meaning "Townland of the Badgers", is a simple two-up, two-down farmhouse with rough-hewn walls of granite, and window

ABOVE: *The blue painted
wall behind these wooden
shelves sets off an eclectic
arrangement of pottery,
including Irish spongeware.
To the left of the chair is a
container for butter knives;
on the right a butter churn
and mixer.*

LEFT: *A "famine chair" (far
left) and a "sugawn" chair
(right) in front of the
original staircase. Patrick
has the true collector's
knack for unexpected finds.
He acquired the contents
of a derelict cottage in
exchange for a couple of
watercolours, and found
the Victorian campaign
chair (centre) on a
skip (dumpster).*

125

BELOW: *Patrick rescued this elegant bedstead from its almost certain fate as part of a cattle fence or gate when he saw it lying by the roadside on the way to Clonmel, County Tipperary.*

OPPOSITE: *The long barn, lit from the conservatory, doubles as a studio. The dining-room table is made from a door.*

mouldings that date the house to about 1830. In typical Irish rural style, the farm buildings were attached to the house, creating a natural extension of the living area into the stables and long barn.

Patrick Scott is one of Ireland's best-known artists, but he resisted the temptation to insert windows in the south-facing side of the barn, which he uses mainly as a studio. When working here in Wicklow he prefers to avoid the distractions of the exterior. Instead he designed and built a cedarwood conservatory next to the long barn which, by trapping whatever sunshine is available, lights and warms the barn. When he is not working, the conservatory is the perfect spot from which to enjoy the Wicklow countryside, whatever the weather.

Patrick decided not to employ professional builders for the conversion, preferring to do as much of the work as possible himself. It took two years for the work to be completed, as floors and ceilings had to be replaced and a century of smoke and grime cleaned from the walls. His next-door neighbour turned out to be an inspired craftsman as well as a farmer.

Afterwards, says Patrick, money was tight, so he had to "scavenge and barter" his way into furnishing his farmhouse. Nearly everything in the cottage was bought for a song in Dublin markets or local sales. What began in the 1960s as a collection of bric-a-brac has become a haven of vanishing country furniture and implements.

VERSIONS OF
THE PASTORAL

GOLA ISLAND

ABOVE: *The deserted island village with Errigal, Ulster's highest mountain, behind.*
OPPOSITE: *An upstairs bedroom with traditional tongue-and-groove ceiling.*

IT WOULD BE DIFFICULT TO FIND A COUPLE who make more adventurous use of their leisure time than Ulster-born architect Nick Groves Raines and his Icelandic wife and partner, Limma. When not practising in Edinburgh, where they have restored two fine old Scottish castles, they head for Gola, a 200-hectare (500-acre) island off the coast of Donegal. Here amid the Atlantic squalls they enjoy a life of perfect seclusion. The people of this once thriving community left their island for a more comfortable existence on the mainland thirty years ago.

Nick and Limma bought their cottage the same year that the last full-time residents left. They had to re-roof and re-floor the house completely, which was back-breaking work. Everything – timber, concrete, slates – had to be brought over by boat and hauled up on foot from the jetty. The work took the family six successive summer holidays.

Life on the island can be daunting. Though the distance from the mainland is short – a mere one and a half kilometres (one mile) or so at low tide – the channel is famously treacherous. When the weather is bad, even a simple shopping trip can be quite an ordeal. But when it clears there can be few more wonderful places on earth, with shafts of light moving restlessly over the water, and illuminating the ancient shapes of the Donegal hills. On its western, Atlantic side, the island has impressive granite cliffs.

VERSIONS OF THE PASTORAL

GOLA ISLAND

BELOW: *A photograph of the original owners hangs beneath the stairs. With little to spend their money on in the pre-war years when fishing brought prosperity, the islanders replaced the old sod-roofed crofts they inherited from their forebears, building well-constructed two-storey houses with slate roofs and timber ceilings and floors. Most of the houses were built in the 1920s and '30s.*

RIGHT: *A turf fire warms the hearth beneath a print of the Virgin Mary. Along with their house Nick and Limma acquired about eight hectares (20 acres) of pasturage in different parts of the island plus a section of bog for fuel which Nick cuts and dries in time-honoured fashion.*

KNOCKALAHARA

OPPOSITE: *View from the dining room into Knockalahara's master bedroom. The dining room was built three years after the old cottage was renovated, and the bedroom was added three years after that. The eighteenth-century painted wooden doors are Indian – probably from Goa – and were bought to offset the soft yellow walls.*

LEFT: *The cottage seen from the track, showing the original seventeenth-century farmhouse. A wildflower specialist instructed Gordon Watson, the owner, to sow the daisy and poppy seeds at night under a full moon, and also told him to put a layer of dry sand on top of the existing soil.*

A SMALL BOREEN (CATTLE TRACK) ambling up the side of a hill defines the setting for Knockalahara, in County Waterford. The track peters out just beyond the grounds. Gordon Watson, an antiques dealer based in London, bought the thatched cottage seven years ago on his second visit to Ireland. After a weekend searching in West Cork, which he rejected as too exposed, he was on his way home when he saw the cottage advertised by a Youghal estate agent. A hunch caused him to hire a driver there and then and he made an offer the very same day.

Although the cottage is not far from the town of Waterford, it sits in one of the most beautiful and least known parts of Ireland. Knockalahara means "the side of a hill", and it commands extensive views over an unspoilt rural landscape leading towards the blue, mysterious Knockmealdown hills. Once the haunt of eagles and wolves, it is here that the last wolf in Ireland is said to have been killed, in 1770. In medieval times, before the Elizabethan plantations, Ireland was famed for the export of wolf-skins. The unfortunate animals were hunted to extinction in the belief that they inherited the souls of humans who rejected the Gospel brought to Ireland by St Patrick.

The cottage was originally a farmhouse and its core is seventeenth-century. Wishing to extend it, Gordon set about trying to find the best builder in the vicinity. After several visits to the pub he noticed that the same three names kept coming up, one belonging to an Englishman. At first Gordon opted for his compatriot "out of shyness", but the

LEFT: *The master bedroom and main sitting room. The ebonized wood day-bed and the bookcases are French neoclassical. The metal-frame bed, which doubles as a huge sofa, was made by the local blacksmith and is based on a French Directoire travelling bed. Under the window to the right a pair of swan-shaped bronze taps sits on a late nineteenth-century Scandinavian cabinet painted in blue and gold.*

BELOW: *Detail of the seating area in the dining room. The shutters on the small windows are painted Nantucket Blue, discovered in the local hardware shop. Late nineteenth-century Moroccan saddlebacks are thrown over the sofa.*

135

OPPOSITE: *The guest bathroom with its ochre limewashed walls and original panelled ceiling. The lead bath was bought in a Paris flea market.* BELOW: *Previously an outbuilding, the guest bedroom still has its eighteenth-century thatch and beams. The bedcover is from Rajasthan. The wooden bedhead comes from an Irish church, and was bought from a local antiques dealer.*

Englishman promptly broke his leg so Gordon employed the second builder on the list, Pat, who, along with his effervescent wife, Dolores, lives locally. This proved a great success. They developed a dialogue: "Pat understood instinctively that I wanted it to look like a rustic eighteenth-century cottage rather than a modern bungalow, which is basically what it is," says Gordon.

Pat and Gordon set about joining the rooms together in the existing structure, incorporating the outside workshop, now one of the guest bedrooms, into the main body of the building. The dining room was added three years later, with large French windows opening on to the garden. Gordon's bedroom, which also serves as a sitting room, was added three years after that. Both the dining room and the main bedroom are made of breezeblocks with a coating of cement and limewash, which has been used extensively both outside and within. Being urban as well as urbane, Gordon insisted on underfloor heating in his bedroom, and Pat has become an expert at laying pipes in wiggly patterns under a thin coating of cement. Gordon finds the result endlessly comforting in winter.

The interior benefitted from a meticulous approach to design. After he bought the cottage, Gordon made a large-scale drawing and divided the space up into rooms. He then made correctly scaled cardboard cut-outs of the furniture he intended for the cottage, and experimented with different positions for it on the scale drawing until everything looked exactly right. Except for one table, none of the furniture has been shifted from its intended place.

VERSIONS OF
THE PASTORAL

CROAGHAN

ABOVE: *Croaghan, taken from Lough Swilly at low tide. The core of the house may have been part of the outer defences of a Stewart castle.*
OPPOSITE: *Sean Rafferty put back the window casings and shutters, which are lined with studded royal blue felt to keep the house warm in winter. On the Moroccan day-bed lies a rug made by McNutt of Downings – celebrated Donegal tweed specialists who supply couturiers all over the world.*

WHEN A FRIEND PERSUADED the BBC presenter Sean Rafferty to look at "a wonderful little cottage" on Lough Swilly, he had no intention of buying. But the image of Croaghan perched on the edge of the waters with its ever-changing light would not go away, and he bought the cottage on impulse. Soon afterwards the roof collapsed. "You don't have a survey done on a romantic impulse," countered Sean to his more practical friends.

Croaghan was probably a small outcrop of the Stewart castle two fields away, built in the seventeenth century to fortify the Stewart estates. The cottage's thick walls and ancient stone staircase, which appears to have been external, suggest defensive purposes. The Stewarts settled in the Lough Swilly area as part of the Ulster plantation scheme of the sixteenth and seventeenth centuries, when land was confiscated from its Irish owners

RIGHT: *View into the conservatory from the exterior window, which is sometimes used as a hatch during parties. Blue Egyptian and turquoise glasses from Biot in Provence catch the light on the window-sill, presided over by the silhouette of a tiger on an Indian candlestick.*

and settled by English and Scots through the agency of colonists known as "undertakers" (because in taking over the land they undertook to settle it with sub-colonists on behalf of the English government). "From Scotland came many, and from England not a few," wrote Andrew Stewart, who took a jaundiced view of his fellow settlers, "yet all of them generally the scum of both nations, who for debt, or breaking and fleeing from justice, in a land where there was nothing, or but little, as yet of the fear of God." The cottage was gentrified in the early nineteenth century, and in the 1930s was used as a duck-shooting lodge. A stone's throw in the opposite direction from the castle, the Ferry House marks the place where the old ferry plied its way across Lough Swilly with livestock and other produce for Derry. Three hundred and fifty years on, the Stewarts still have local connections. Sir Alan, a boat-builder, lives in nearby Ramelton, and his son Lindsay made a table for Sean, to go in the cottage.

ABOVE: *Sean added the conservatory/dining room to create more space. "The pleasure of eating is greatly enhanced by the shifting kaleidoscope of light on the water," says Sean. He chose the powder-blue woodwork "because it merges with the sky when it's blue and on a grey day stands out against it".*

LEFT: *The dresser was made by the local carpenter from an old carved oak sideboard supported by two scrolls from a redundant piano. A pot-pourri of pottery stands out against the Provençal blue painted boards.*

CAPARD

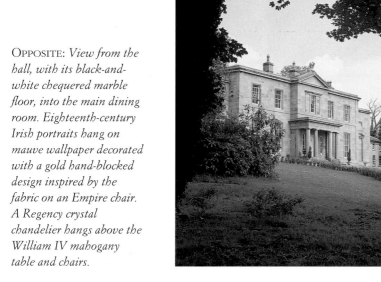

OPPOSITE: *View from the hall, with its black-and-white chequered marble floor, into the main dining room. Eighteenth-century Irish portraits hang on mauve wallpaper decorated with a gold hand-blocked design inspired by the fabric on an Empire chair. A Regency crystal chandelier hangs above the William IV mahogany table and chairs.*

LEFT: *From its elevated position Capard commands an extensive view over rolling countryside. The house was built in 1798. The smaller annex to the right of the house has been turned into guest quarters.*

CAPARD SITS ON A LOFTY EMINENCE on the edge of the Slieve Bloom Mountains in County Laois. As soon as Tom Dobson saw it, he knew it was absolutely right. "The beauty of Capard," says Tom, "is that it looks monumental from the outside, but inside it is easy to live in, with well-proportioned, but not too grand, rooms." There were other advantages, too. Tom is in the antiques business and needed to be within an hour or so of Dublin, but he also wished to live in a truly rural landscape. The magnificent views from the house over rolling countryside must also have swayed him.

Capard was built in 1798 for one John Piggott, on the site of a previously demolished eighteenth-century castellated house that had been erected on the site of a sixteenth-century tower house burnt down in 1738. Mr Piggott employed two hundred people and carried out a carefully orchestrated programme of planting, which included oaks, beeches, limes and sequoias behind the house. Many fine trees are still there today.

When Tom discovered the house, it had been sadly neglected and the windows had been shuttered for many years. The only inhabitants were two elderly retainers, Maggie and Eddie Kenny, whose father had been the butler at Capard until his death in 1967. Maggie and Eddie, now well into their eighties, once went to school on the estate and worked in the house where, to this moment, they pass the day in the old kitchen, keeping it warm and cheerful for Tom's return in the evening. When there are no guests the three of them often cook and eat together.

RESTORATION AND REVIVAL

CAPARD

RIGHT: *The yellow drawing room – formerly the laundry room. The mahogany and oak inlaid floor was found in a salvage yard. A pair of eighteenth-century oval gilt mirrors hang above gilt tables with Irish inlaid-marble tops. The 7.5-metre (25-foot) Regency curtain rail came from a house in Carlow.*

BELOW: *The poppy-red dining room is used for intimate supper parties. Over an Irish sideboard hangs a Chinese Chippendale gilt mirror and a collection of eighteenth-century oval pastels. The table is set with an Italian dinner service, French silver-gilt cutlery and Irish Waterford crystal.*

ABOVE: *The blue dining room in the guest wing has a 1750s Kilkenny marble fireplace. The oval dining table with side flaps is an eighteenth-century Irish hunt table or coffin table – its alternative names reflect its dual function of bearing drinks at a hunt meet and supporting the coffin at a wake.*

Restoring the house would have daunted most people, but Tom is a man with a mission. His energy and joviality are such that the inevitable setbacks are forgotten in his exhilarating enthusiasm. After Tom had restored and decorated the main part of the house he turned his energies to the servants' quarters, which housed the laundry rooms, tack room and storerooms, and converted them into a wing for his guests.

The interior decoration suggests more than a hint of theatre. Tom is exacting in his requirements and meticulous in execution. In his choice of colours he is fastidious to a degree. Seven attempts were made by "a very patient painter" before Tom was satisfied with the warm blue in the guest dining room. The bright yet soft effect he sought in the summer drawing room was finally achieved by copying the yellow in a Bacchanalian scene after Poussin, which hangs above the mantelpiece in the same room. Most telling was the source of inspiration for the colour of the wallpaper in the main dining room. "Although

the hand-blocked design originally came from a green Empire chair," says Tom, "I wanted a more imperial purple. Eventually I found the exact colour on the inside page of a Christie's catalogue of jade in Hong Kong." They commissioned the paper and had the blocks specially made.

Irrepressible, Tom has now turned his energies to the demesne. The stables higher up the hill have been re-roofed and are now home to five horses who take Tom and his guests trekking in the Slieve Bloom Mountains. The former pleasure gardens, originally created by John Piggott, are being renovated and extended. In the old walled garden a historical rose garden takes shape. At the end of the straight canal built for the previous house in the 1730s, a temple is being made from reconstituted stone, echoing the pedimented break-front and Ionic porch of the house. And, far from exhausting his zeal for restoration on Capard, Tom has just rescued a crumbling Palladian villa not far away.

ABOVE: *View from the hall of the guest wing through the drawing room to the blue dining room. The shouldered door casing was rescued from an eighteenth-century Dublin house. Standing against the wall of the drawing room are two Irish giltwood sofas, and at the end of the room is an Irish inlaid marble fireplace.*

149

RESTORATION AND REVIVAL

ARLANDS INCH

ABOVE: *Arlands Inch viewed from the bridge in Thomastown. While the mill dates back to medieval times, the present structure is probably late eighteenth-century. The Somerville-Larges bought the mill in 1994.*
OPPOSITE: *The hall, with its painted chequered wooden floor. The pictures include one of a pair of engravings of dead birds by Edouard Travies (top left) and a Tibetan thankgka (right), used as a Buddhist aid to meditation.*

ONCE THERE WERE HALF A DOZEN WORKING MILLS on the River Nore at Thomastown in County Kilkenny. After a Norman knight, Thomas FitzAnthony, founded the town in the thirteenth century, milling in all its guises became the main industry. The steady turn of water-wheels must have seemed eternal. These days the mills have other uses: one is a craft centre, while another houses an art gallery. Arlands Inch, which like the other mills has medieval foundations, became the offices of a central heating firm which left behind many comforting radiators. Later it became the improbable setting for an international centre for Russian performing arts.

Today Arlands Inch is the home of Peter and Gillian Somerville-Large, both of them authors. Related to Edith Somerville, the Irish novelist and illustrator who co-authored

RESTORATION AND REVIVAL

ARLANDS INCH

RIGHT: *The main gallery runs the whole length of the mill. Peter painted the design on the wooden floor. The model ship on the left is a Galway hooker, and two Chinese hangings rescued from the siege of Peking hang at the end.*

BELOW: *Detail of the drawing room with the landing and stairs beyond. A floor was taken out to give the rooms higher ceilings. The Neapolitan scene above the double doors is said to have been brought from France by a Royalist lady refugee who lived in Cork with Peter's family.*

ABOVE: *Although the mill has central heating, the Wellington stove burns throughout the winter. The bookcase was made locally.*

RIGHT: *A kelim covers a large rustic table in the dining room. The stamped leather Spanish screen came from Abbeyleix House in County Laois. The ceiling beams are decorated with two pieces of carved wood – one with an oak motif which came from Dublin and the other a painted carving from a Russian iconostasis (icon-bearing screen).*

154

the "Irish RM" stories, Peter has written ten books about Ireland, as well as several other books inspired by his travels in Nepal, Tibet, Afghanistan and the Middle East.

The Somerville-Larges had lived in numerous other houses before buying the mill. Many factors enticed them to Arlands Inch – the sound of water, the sight of the salmon leaping the weir, and most of all the majestic sweep of the river, where nothing is static. The mill dweller is forever aware of the changes wrought by water and weather.

Over the years Arlands Inch has absorbed a pot-pourri of the couple's possessions – some inherited from family, others collected on their travels. The Somerville-Larges have a knack of putting objects together in small "vignettes" as if, grouped together, they can measure up against the huge expanses of white wall.

Every aspect of the landscape recalls the Normans. The view east from the couple's bedroom looks over water meadows to the town, with its medieval wall, broken towers and castle guarding the humped bridge. Also visible are the remains of another castle, built by Thomas FitzAnthony on a prehistoric site. On the south side of the river, just out of sight, stand the ruins of the Cistercian Abbey of Jerpoint.

On fine summer evenings, drink in hand, one can recline on the balcony overlooking the river and watch the birds – the daily heron, the swallows and martins, the dippers and the cormorants. Sometimes a kingfisher flashes by. There is always bread for the swans. Occasionally a fisherman leaves a gift of trout outside the door. When a salmon is caught, the whole world gets to hear about it.

ABOVE: *An eighteenth-century French armoire flanked by two painted chairs stands in front of an Armenian carpet from Lake Van in eastern Turkey.*

155

RESTORATION AND REVIVAL

PREHEN

ABOVE: *Parts of Prehen date back to the 1640s and from its vantage point above the Foyle overlooking Derry city, the house must have witnessed many a scene of strife. The eighteenth-century front has handsome windows with rusticated surrounds and a Greek revival pedimented door.*
OPPOSITE: *Carola Peck painted the frescoes in the dining room at Prehen for a party. The mahogany side table is Irish.*

"WE APPROACHED THE FORMER KNOX HOME and found it in a state of dilapidation. I pushed open the door and it almost fell from its hinges. The floors had been torn out in many places, and great openings showed where magnificent fireplaces once stood. Bare rafters marked the spots where, in former days, fine eighteenth-century ceilings met the eye of the beholder." So wrote a curious visitor, Hugh McVeigh, who as a child had picked wild flowers in the surrounding woods while listening to his father's tales of the once great house.

A stone's throw from the city of Derry, Prehen dates from the mid-eighteenth century, and incorporates an older, seventeenth-century building constructed during the reign of Charles I. Local tradition has it that during the siege of Derry in 1689, when the

Right: The Marriage of Isaac and Rebecca, *after Claude Lorraine, hangs above a carved gilt cupboard – part of a set of Pondicherry furniture from Castletown (qv).*

Below: *The saloon, with a view through to the stair landing. The peacock-blue walls are copied from the Chinese room at Carton in County Kildare. The oval portraits in contemporary frames are (left) William III and (right) his friend the Duke of Portland.*

Protestant Apprentice Boys locked the gates of the city and held out for over a hundred days against the forces of the Catholic King James II, Jacobite irregulars stripped Prehen of its panelling for firewood. At the time the house belonged to Alderman Tomkins, whose family originally owned the Prehen estate. With the marriage in 1740 of his granddaughter, Honoria, to Colonel Andrew Knox, MP, the house passed into the Knox family. The Colonel's only daughter, Mary Ann, became a tragic *cause célèbre* when she was shot dead in her coach by a suitor, John MacNaughton, whom she had spurned in marriage. As the murderer was being hanged, the rope broke, and he had to be hanged a second time. To this day he is known in the vicinity as "half-hung MacNaughton".

In 1910 George Von Scheffler, a Prussian, inherited Prehen from his maternal grandfather, Lieutenant-Colonel George Knox. Von Scheffler loved the house and planned to live there; he even added Knox to his name. But when the First World War

ABOVE: *Caroline houses usually had an upper-floor saloon opening into the bedrooms, as shown here. The bed came from Ardgillan Castle in County Dublin. In the foreground a portrait of James II hangs above a gilt table and to the right is a section of an elaborate carved screen.*

RIGHT: *An Irish mahogany table stands in front of the assembled gilt-decorated bookcases in the library. The Spanish leather screen on the left is made from seventeenth-century wall coverings from Shelton Abbey, County Wicklow.*
BELOW: *Dutch marquetry furniture is shown to good advantage against the saffron walls of this guest bedroom.*

broke out, Prehen was seized by the British government as enemy property and auctioned. Though prevented from inheriting his property, Von Scheffler continued to regard Ireland as his home; when he died, "Come Back to Erin" was played at his cremation in Hamburg, and his ashes were brought to Derry to be interred.

The present owner, Julian Peck, is descended from another branch of the Ulster Knox family. When Julian and Carola Peck bought Prehen in 1971, during the height of the "Troubles", the only reason for its survival was a preservation order. New housing had encroached to within 180 metres (200 yards) of the front door. With heroic dedication the Pecks set about the renovation, scrubbing off layers of encrusted paint. In rooms where ornamental strapwork was discovered, the walls were painted a distressed white. Elsewhere Carola Peck used strong Georgian colours, reflecting the influence of Mariga Guinness at Leixlip Castle and Castletown (*qqv*).

ABOVE: *The dramatic use of the complementary colours red-orange and blue-green in the Empire bedroom creates an eye-catching effect. On the wall to the right of the French Empire bed hangs a French colour print from the 1820s. All the other furniture and artefacts in the room are from the same period.*

FEDANY

ABOVE: *The schoolhouse, built in the 1870s, with the two-storey schoolmaster's house,*
a later addition, on the right.
OPPOSITE: *At Fedany, the whole living area is contained within the former schoolroom.*
In the foreground is an eighteenth-century games table. The watercolours to the right of
the chimney-breast are scenes of Donegal painted by the governess to the Earls
of Leitrim in the nineteenth century.

THE APPROACH TO FEDANY REVEALS few of the delights awaiting the visitor on entering the house. Crossing the threshhold of the grey-stoned, slate-roofed building into the main living room is a genuine surprise. By contrast with the modest exterior, the room appears enormous and everything in it suggests longevity of tenure. Nothing jars, nothing offends and the sense of calm that overtakes the visitor is immeasurably enhanced by the warm, diffuse light. It is easy to understand why Amanda Douglas, an interior designer based in London, was captivated. Commissioned by clients to find and renovate a small house in the Irish countryside, she had searched extensively for over a year before discovering the house in the depths of rural Cork.

The situation is charming – a quiet, secluded spot by a stream, in the fold between two hill farms, with gently rolling pastures of sheep and cattle. Fedany – which, according to

Joyce's *Irish Names of Places* (1875) is derived from the Gaelic word *feadánach,* meaning "a streamy place" – was originally a schoolhouse built in the late nineteenth century for the Protestant children of Cornish miners brought over to work the now extinct copper mines. A two-storey dwelling for the schoolmaster was later added to one end.

When Amanda found the property, the building was in a sad and parlous state, having been empty for thirty-six years. The exterior walls were hidden behind a thick layer of brambles and the inside was not much better. The ground floor of the schoolmaster's house was filled with toilet cubicles and the only way to reach the upper rooms was by way of a rickety ladder from the corner of what is now the study. But Amanda was impressed by the size of the classroom and immediately recognized its potential – despite the fact that it was painted a hideous orange and had an old wood-burning stove in the middle. "The room had a wonderful feel about it, although it was in a tragic state," she says. The open-beamed wooden roof was intact and so was the tongue-and-groove wainscoting. Despite her clients' limited budget, Amanda saw that she could achieve something distinctive, and that the house would be easy and inexpensive to run. The building work was completed in just six months. For reasons of economy the clients refrained from using a licensed architect and employed instead a local builder under Amanda's supervision.

Amanda planned the garden with landscape gardener Robert Myerscough. The warm Gulf Stream has created a frost-free micro-climate in which exotic subtropical plants like

ABOVE: *The guest
bedroom has an Edwardian
brass bed with a paisley
cover and an antique
hanging, found by
Amanda.*

ABOVE LEFT: *A gilt-
framed oval portrait of a
young woman hangs
above the Victorian
mantelpiece, which has a
Staffordshire china figurine
at each end. The fireplace is
covered by an antique
découpage firescreen.*

palms, fern-trees and giant bamboos can survive. A stream was diverted to flow through the property and has provided an opportunity to plant many rare water plants in the wild part of the garden. Anticipating the need for a small private area, they surrounded the house with a beech hedge, which has now matured.

The 12-metre (40-foot) schoolroom presented a challenge. It was decided that the best way to treat it was to combine the activities of cooking, eating and relaxing in the same large space. "Who wants to be banished to the kitchen when everyone else is having a good *craic*?" comments Amanda. "The way we've done it, the cook can join in the fun." There is a kitchen at the window end, a dining room near the middle and a sitting room, centred around the fireplace, at the opposite end. The kitchen has built-in wooden cupboards and drawers, painted white, which support a beechwood work surface running the length of the wall and incorporating the range.

The clean lines of the room's structure combine with a clever use of furniture and fabrics to create an elegant yet comfortable effect, enhanced by the delicate shade of the wall, which acts as a foil for the pictures. Blue-and-white checked curtains stretched behind chicken wire have replaced the cupboard door panels in the kitchen area. The same material is used, in the traditional Irish cottage way, along the lower shelf to conceal the strip lights mounted under the shelf. The colours are repeated in striped curtains, upholstered sofas and the kitchen cushions, where the fabric has been turned inside out to achieve a subtler, more faded effect. The combination of Irish furniture and paintings,

OPPOSITE: *The
schoolroom, looking
towards the kitchen area.*
BELOW: *Two early
nineteenth-century
portraits hang above a
sturdy eighteenth-century
Irish table.*

huge vases of flowers and foliage, bowls of pot-pourri and ever-present books creates that special and hard-to-define sense of ease and timelessness so characteristic of Irish country homes.

It was one such house – Rossanagh in County Wicklow, home to Amanda's great-aunt – that moulded the designer's taste. "Rossanagh influenced me profoundly," she remembers from childhood visits. "It was wonderfully big and full of tatty bits of furniture, some of it rather grand: there were lots of books and flowers and faded chintzes and it was altogether more chaotic and relaxed than an English country house."

But it was Mariga Guinness, with whom Amanda worked at Castletown (*qv*) for the Irish Georgian Society, who made her appreciate the art of interior design. As Amanda explains, "She was the first person I saw putting everything together from scratch, striving always for what she called 'this wonderful look'."

CORKE LODGE

LEFT: *Corke Lodge,
designed in 1840 by James
Shiel, has been given a
dual personality – austere
neoclassical in front
and romantic Gothic
behind. This playfulness
appeals to its present
owner, the architect
and designer Alfred
Cochrane, who revels in
post-modern eclecticism.*

OPPOSITE: *The view from
the drawing room through
the hall to the dining room
at the end. Painted white
floors and delicate pale
colours create a sense of
light and spaciousness. The
console table, one of
Alfred's "zoomorphic"
designs, stands in front of
a panoramic mural
depicting imaginary
Mediterranean landscapes.*

ORKE LODGE, NEAR THE IRISH SEASIDE TOWN of Bray, County
Wicklow, is an architectural tease. To the outside world it presents an
elegant, if slightly austere, neoclassical façade. But the private, garden
side has a romantic Gothic revival look, enhanced by the evergreens –
ilexes, yews and a cork tree – that lead into the surrounding
woodlands. The same dichotomy is reflected in the interior. The front
rooms have lofty ceilings with classical detailing; those on the garden side have Gothic
windows and fireplaces.

The house was built around 1840 by one of Ireland's wealthiest women, Louisa
Mangan, on the burned-out ruins of an earlier country house. Designed by James Shiel,
Ireland's most fashionable Regency architect, it made a witty comment on the
architectural debate between neoclassicists and Gothic-revivalists by having the best of
both worlds. It seems doubtful, however, that its principal owner, Louisa's daughter
Georgina Augusta, ever enjoyed her mother's little architectural conceit. Jilted by her
fiancé on the eve of her wedding, Ireland's most sought-after heiress retired to her
country estates in County Westmeath, never to be seen again in Dublin or Bray. A famous
recluse, she is thought to have been the prototype for Miss Haversham in Charles
Dickens's *Great Expectations*.

After Miss Mangan's death in 1905, Corke Lodge and the estate were bought by a
neighbour, Sir Stanley Cochrane, great-uncle of its present owner, the architect and

ABOVE: *An 1870s
Romantic Gothic landscape
by Francis Krause hangs
above the original painted
mantelpiece designed by
architect James Shiel.
Alfred bought the brass
curtain poles for a four-
poster bed, but used them
instead as decoration for
his clothes cupboards.*

RIGHT: *Of the library
Alfred says, "Four alcoves
were created by using
carved-oak surrounds in
the Hiberno–Romanesque
style of the 1850s." The
seventeenth-century
wood-carvings are
North European.*

designer Alfred Cochrane. Since then it has been part of the Woodbrook estate, now owned by Alfred's elder brother, Sir Marc. As a second home on the family property, it suffered from benign neglect, housing guests or widowed aunts. During the heyday of Bray's famous Ardmore Studios in the 1950s, illustrious tenants included the actresses Geraldine FitzGerald and Katharine Hepburn.

When Alfred Cochrane inherited Corke Lodge in 1979, he immediately embarked on much-needed repairs. "Much of the exterior gothickry had rotted away," he explains. "I decided to replace it with similar granite elements from nearby Glendalough House, a Gothic mansion that was being demolished. There was such a quantity of salvaged stone that the temptation to extend the garden front was irresistible. So I added a winter garden/conservatory, as well as a cloister to store logs in. The conservatory provides shelter for guests and food should a summer cloudburst interrupt a garden party."

In restoring the interior, Cochrane has paid homage to James Shiel's conception without slavishly being bound by his original design. The ground floor has been extensively remodelled. The original staircase, afflicted by dry rot, was moved sideways to create an axial vista from the front door into the garden. "I designed the new staircase, with its grid of mirrored and blue pillared screens, as a post-modern homage to the classical, represented by the eighteenth-century marble statue of a dancing faun," says Cochrane. "Then I transformed the front drawing room into an Italian loggia with real pilasters and *trompe l'oeil* plants."

ABOVE: *Alfred insists that the bed in his room, raised on a three-step dais, was created "not out of megalomania, but to be above the draft caused by an open fire". Alfred's initial hanging above the bed is repeated in the bedspread. The room has a medieval theme, with cupboards painted to simulate tent walls.*

171

ABOVE: *Most of the modern furniture was designed by Alfred for his "Alfrank" line. His winged-lion Babylonian chair is a prototype for the gold-leafed steel designs used for the Equus lamp on the table.*

RIGHT: *The glass panels flanking the chimney-breast in the Italianate drawing room help to bring the garden into the room. The exotic effect is accentuated by clever planting of bamboos and palms, and the* trompe l'oeil *plants around the walls. A collection of architectural prints hangs above the mantelpiece.*

172

BELOW: *The dining room
has painted white floors
and walls and a large
transparent table supported
by Ionic pillars designed by
Alfred. The* faux marbre
*architraves and skirting
emphasize the architectural
elements in the room.
Italian candlesticks stand
on the Regency sideboard.*

Vistas were opened on either side of the fireplace and planted with palms and other flora. "I think it subconsciously reflects the views from our house in Beirut," says Cochrane, whose mother is Lebanese. The Beit Sursock, where he and his family lived when not in Ireland, was a fine old palace in the Ottoman style, with a plant-filled courtyard and splendid views of the Mediterranean coast.

To James Shiel's architectural fantasy Cochrane added his own playful, post-modern variations, blending antique with modern furniture. "I inherited more decorative objects and paintings than useful tables and chairs; so I bought some late Regency, William IV and early Victorian pieces that were contemporary with Corke Lodge and appropriately architectural or exotic." To this he has added pieces of his own design. In the dining room, the white walls, floor and ceiling draw attention to the main architectural features – the architraves and unusually large pillared mantelpiece, picked out in marbling as if suspended in space.

In contrast to the ground floor, the upstairs rooms are painted in warm colours to provide a comfortable refuge from the long, damp Irish winters. "I wanted the upstairs layout of the house to suit winter hibernation for one or two people, leaving the ground floor free for large-scale entertaining," says Cochrane. The library/living room is on the

Gothic side of the house. A collection of seventeenth-century German carvings over the mantelpiece conveys the same monastic message as the garden façade from the outside. A brass deer that holds logs suggests a hunting lodge. Four alcoves with carved wooden surrounds – salvaged from the Church of the Holy Redeemer in nearby Bray – complete the effect. "It's designed as a hermitage," says Cochrane, "a cosy, self-contained place in which to pass a long winter."

Eclecticism is second-nature to Alfred Cochrane. "Even as a child I dreamed of owning Corke Lodge," he says. His dream came true and he was free at last to indulge his architectural tastes. Though much in demand as an architect and designer – his business frequently takes him to London and places further afield – he sometimes chafes at the restrictions of his trade. "In my own home," he says, "I can try out the tricks that none of my clients would ever dare let me play in theirs."

ABOVE: *Real plants intermingle with painted green foliage to create a lusciously tropical effect in the conservatory, enhanced by the hammock. A fragment of a carved Ionic capital is reflected in the glass table, and on the left stands a chaise longue covered with ticking.*

INDEX

Figures in italics refer to illustration captions